UWE BOLL RAW: A MEMOIR

UWE BOLL RAW:
A MEMOIR

Uwe Boll

BearManor Media

2024

Published in the United States of America by:

BearManor Media

1317 Edgewater Dr. #110
Orlando, FL 32804

bearmanormedia.com

Printed in the United States.

Typesetting and layout by PKJ Passion Global

ISBN–979-8-88771-539-1

Advance Praise for Uwe Boll Raw: A Memoir

"I admire my friend, Uwe... He's always done it 'his way.'" - Clint Howard

"I loved working with Uwe, he answered to no one and loves making movies, the definition of independent filmmaker!" - Michael Paré

"Working with Uwe has been a remarkable journey. He truly allows his actors to be creative, participating in the development behind the world we bring to life. Uwe approaches each project with an open mind and heart, allowing for a remarkable collaborative creative process." - Kristen Renton

"Uwe makes no apologies for his work nor for his clear points of view. He operates fearlessly in a fear-driven business while showing the utmost respect and open mindedness, in the true spirit of a collaborator, to his fellow artists." - Daniel Serafini-Sauli

"Uwe is the most 'fuck it all' of all the directors that I've worked with. He doesn't surrender to people's opinions and the industry's ways of doing things.

When I directed my first film I bumped into Lars Von Trier at Zentropa, and I boldly asked him what advice he'd give a new director. He said, "Don't listen to anyone," and then wandered off. I know exactly what he meant!

I failed to follow his advice, but I can see that Uwe has not... He's doing exactly that, and that's what gives him a unique artist's voice. He also lets the actors have the freedom to improvise and participate, which of course for any actor makes it so much more fun, but it also makes you humble when a director will trust all that you can add to the finished product." - Ulrich Thomsen

"I would work with Uwe Boll on a drop of a dime. I love him." - Amanda Plummer

Contents

FOREWORD

If nothing else, Uwe Boll is resilient. Through a career spanning over three decades, Uwe has made films spanning nearly every genre imaginable. Whether you are looking for horror (*Seed* (2006)), satire (*Postal* (2007)), or a thriller (*Blackwoods* (2001)), Dr. Boll has you covered.

In *Uwe Boll Raw: A Memoir*, you'll learn a different side of the man than you probably have read about in the press. He's not a madman. He's not the worst filmmaker of all time. Instead, he's a person just like you or me, albeit a more successful one.

Much like his films, Dr. Boll is more complicated than one might assume at first glance. There are very personal insights in here about the current state of filmmaking, the environment, and the perils of running a restaurant. Yes, there's also the entertaining behind-the-scenes stories of his films which fans have come to expect from his raucous DVD commentaries, but this book is also about how Boll lives his life.

I have a feeling this memoir, his first in English, will surprise people.

Mat Bradley-Tschirgi (Author, *The Films of Uwe Boll Vol 1: The Video Game Movies (2003-2014)*

PROLOGUE

On the first day of shooting *BloodRayne* (2005) in Romania, Shawn Williamson's advice to replace Michael Madsen echoed in my ears. Similarly, Christian Slater urged me to dismiss Tara Reid during the *Alone in the Dark* (2005) shoot. Regrettably, I chose to ignore their counsel, convinced I had valid reasons. Looking back, I realize my decisions were flawed.

During *Alone in the Dark*, Tara Reid's significant sales value from the success of *American Pie* (1999) was undeniable. Firing her meant losing that value and finding a replacement within 24 hours was improbable. On *BloodRayne*, shooting in Romania posed logistical challenges in swiftly replacing an American or British actor. Fearful of exceeding the budget by halting production on the first day, I hesitated. As Clint Howard later noted in an interview, "Uwe is the director and producer. He has that struggle between the producer and the director in him… The Producer wins!"

In hindsight, firing both actors would have been the wiser choice, replacing them with capable actors. Madsen's refusal to leave his wardrobe and his disruptive behavior on set should have warranted his dismissal. Reid, a kind person, struggled with her role in *Alone in the Dark*, turning the character into a joke. I should have made the difficult decision to let her go.

My struggles as a director and producer are chronicled in three books in Germany (*Ihr könnt mich mal!* (2017), *Warum sich keiner mehr zu sagen traut was wirklich ist* (2022), and *Tabula Rasa* (2023)) detailing my life, work, ideas, and political views. Now, with this book *Uwe Boll Raw: A Memoir*, it's time to share these experiences with my global audience in English.

Despite an upbringing that wasn't particularly unhappy, spectacular, or dangerous, a prevailing sense of dissatisfaction lingered in me. The dream of becoming a film director seemed unattainable due to my lack of financial resources and connections in the film and TV industry.

EVERY BEGINNING IS HARD or SHIT

"If you don't want it happen to you, don't do it to anyone else!" is completely sufficient as moral compass for everybody." – *Lutheran Bible* circa 1545

I'm a sporty, successful, and humorous boy from a lower-middle-class family in the tranquil Bergisches Land mountain range in West Germany. I earned a doctorate in literature and an unparalleled career as a film director, writer and producer. I've made over 36 international films as a director and producer with a production volume of around $500 million. I raised all that money myself from German investors. I even went public in the Entry Standard stock market in Frankfurt, founding my own worldwide film sales agency Event Films, which has made over 5,400 sales contracts to date.

I have created and moved things like hardly anyone else came from a similar upbringing. There was no money or contacts from Parents, relatives, or acquaintances. I was entirely a self-made man, a boy from Burscheid who decided to become a director at the tender age of 10. My films are shown in all countries of the world, often in the cinema, but are always available on DVD, TV, and streaming services. And yet, I'm also an aggressive, impatient, cynical, envious guy who is never satisfied. I think that I never got credit for all that I did.

I was born in Wermelskirchen on June 22, 1965, in the Rheinisch-Bergisch district in West Germany, which is close to Cologne. I was raised in Burscheid and went to primary school in Dierath. As for high school, I went to Leverkusen, first to Ina Seidel, then later to Werner Heisenberg. My mother, Erna (everyone only called her Erni) was a housewife. My father, Manfred, was a chemical technician at Bayer Leverkusen, the chemical giant. There was only one brother, Stefan, who was four-and-a-half years older than me.

As expected, I got the short end of the stick in arguments. Once, I even threw a knife at him, and he fended it off with a chair. We played table tennis, soccer, handball, squash, and tennis. Our duels, even when racing, were always tough. The older I got, the more I was able to win. My childhood and youth were shaped by playing sports and watching films.

In Burscheid, there was a cinema that showed classics at the matinee every Sunday for the entry fee of a single German mark. When I was six years old, I already went alone to that cinema to see films like *Ben-Hur* (1959), *Doctor Zhivago* (1965), *Godzilla* (1954), and many more! Many boys in the neighborhood were not allowed to go to the movies, so I told them the film's stories. They were all fascinated by my storytelling, and that I was even allowed to watch the films in the first place. The Burscheider Cinema went bankrupt when I was 10. From then on, I had to take the bus to Leverkusen-Opladen in order to be able to see films in the cinema. After a few years, I made a deal with the Scala Cinema… I made a program flyer for them every week. In exchange, I got free entry whenever I wanted and even earned a few marks for making the flyers.

My mother's Parents, Grandma Sophie and Grandpa Karl, died when I was very young. This was also the case with my father's father, August, but my father's mother, Grandma Hertha, was alive for my whole childhood. She lived right around the corner from us. Every Saturday, I slept over at her house, and she let me watch TV till midnight. Every Saturday night, classic Western movies would play. I watched *El Dorado* (1966), *Rio Bravo* (1959), *Winchester 73* (1950), *The Man Who Shot Liberty Valance* (1962), and loved them all. I also always mowed her lawn for 10 marks. and she starred in my first film *German Fried Movie* (1991). She's even on the poster of the film with the Patriot missile in her hand! A few years after *German Fried Movie* came out, she died of colon cancer at home, refusing an operation. She died in great pain. While this was happening, I was in Kuwait with Frank Lustig raising money for the feature *I Was Saddam's Son* (2013).

Twenty years later, interviewers would always ask me if there was a specific film that made me want to be a film director. My answer to this was always the same, *Mutiny on the Bounty* (1962) starring Marlon Brando. When I was 10, I thought that as a film director, you somehow experienced all the adventures that you see in a film. Of course, the film was great, full of beach, boats, and beautiful women! Was it the reality of filmmaking? No, but at that time, I thought it was.

GOD, RELIGION, CHURCHES

As Karl Marx aptly put it, "Religion is opium for the people."

My views on religion remained skeptical, rooted in a rational perspective.

God doesn't exist! Well, let me put it this way… There is nothing to suggest that there is one God or multiple gods. In the last few centuries, natural sciences have already refuted an extremely large number of religious matters and with increasing scientific clarification. At some point, even the last miracles and mysteries prove to be total bullshit. Because people are very emotionally structured, there are always religions and all sorts of cults that exploit and exclude people; at the same time, they give people support and comfort. Churches have committed incredible crimes throughout history, but they are now anchored in society and have taken over many social services.

Expropriating the churches only makes sense if the state can then offer the social services for better or cheaper. There are tens of thousands of books on this topic, and I would like to finish my chapter in the good old Uwe Boll manner… How stupid do you have to be to run after a god or a cult leader? If there was a god, he certainly wouldn't need us; see my film *Postal* for more on this topic.

I find deeply religious individuals, including celebrities like Tom Cruise and John Travolta, to be somewhat misguided. A simple moral principle, treat others as you want to be treated, is sufficient for navigating life positively.

My Parents were evangelical Christians, but only my mother believed in God. After my confirmation when I was 14 years old, I left the church. The 2,400 DM that I got on my confirmation day was spent for a stereo system and a Ciao moped, which drove 50 km/h (faster as normal mopeds) because my buddy Peter Kiebel drilled the muffler out. The police stopped me three times, but they could never find anything. Because of the moped, I didn't just drive to school (Werner Heisenberg Gymnasium in Leverkusen), but also to the Scala Cinema in Opladen and even the UFA Palast in Cologne. I forged my student ID when I was 15 so that I could get into films rated FSK 16 or above (the equivalent of an R rating). I saw everything from contemporary films at the time like *Friday the 13th* (1980), *Mother's Day* (1980), *Man-Eater* (1980), but also caught classic like Ingmar Bergmann's *Wild Strawberries* (1957).

I was never a good student. Biology, math, and chemistry classes were all boring as shit. I only excelled at sports, social sciences, and sometimes German literature or history. After the 6th grade, the teachers wanted to send me to a lower-end school, but I wanted to go to university, so I insisted on being able to stay at the gymnasium, a higher-end high school.

In Germany, 98% of schools are public and they cost nothing; the same goes for universities. Germany's high school system is a bit different. We have three different kinds of high schools. Hauptschule is for low-end students who will leave school at 15 and learn a job or join the workforce. Realschule is where you leave at 16 and mostly learn a trade like carpenter, bank teller, or electrician. Gymnasium is where you go through grade 13 and then you can go onto a university.

I stayed put in the gymnasium, and I always managed to pass my classes, finally graduating with a 2.9 average. In Germany, the grading works a bit different. 1.0 is the best, and 6 is the absolute worst. Everything higher than a 4 will disqualify you from going to university.

I went to handball training three to four times a week, starting in Hilgen, Wermelskirchen and then later playing in Bergisch Gladbach and Bergisch Neukirchen from the district league up to the Oberliga. I always earned a few hundred marks a month, whether as a player or as a player and coach. When I was 18, I went into the boxing department in addition with Bayer 04 Leverkusen, where I trained for many years. Between the ages of 20 to 28, I had several hundred sparring matches and seven real bouts. I was in top shape at the time! I could run 100 meters in under 12 seconds, complete 160 one-armed push-ups, and finish 50 pull-ups with no problem at all.

In every sport, I was very fast and dynamic, but also always small and not technically perfect. In my first boxing match, I had a 1.92-meter-tall opponent. I am only 1.74 meters tall myself. At first, he boxed me out completely for a round and a half, but then he caught a full right hook from me and fell out of the ring into the spectators. He remained unconscious for five minutes. I won all my fights with stoppages, even if there were only a few. Since we had great trainers, great fighters came into our ranks, including world champions Darius Michalczewski (The Tiger) and Felix Sturm.

I also made a boxing documentary titled *Boxing* (1994), but it looked very unprofessional because we shot on S-VHS, VHS, Beta-max, and Video 2000. Before making that documentary, I sometimes shot on Super 8mm; these were mostly films in which I burned Action Team characters or blew up Revell ships.

Frank, one of my friends from school, wanted to make movies like me. I knew that if we wanted to film something that could be broadcast, then we had to shoot on 16mm, 35mm, or Beta SP. All of those formats were expensive to shoot in. Frank's father had more money than my Parents, so they could support him better. I earned money mowing the lawn, playing handball, worked during school and semester holidays, and saved all my pocket money.

When I was 15 years old, I often rode my bike through the town of Burscheid, collecting bottles to return to the supermarket for extra money. Nevertheless, I also spent money on things such as my record collection. I had most of the albums by Thin Lizzy, Deep Purple, Rainbow, Manfred Man, Supertramp, Yes, and Billy Joel.

Later on, Frank and I shot some commercials on 35mm for a diner, a restaurant, a car dealer, and a waterski hangout. At the same time, I did my community service at the Burscheider ASB as a mobile social assistant and ambulance driver; the salary was not bad at 700 DM per month.

My first car was a VW Beetle, which I bought for 800 marks. I failed the practical driving test two times like an idiot because I was driving too fast, but finally I got my license. During my first winter driving, my tires were completely worn out. Since my car lacked a proper heater, I saw almost nothing when I was driving. One day, my car slipped into the wall of the house right next to the police station. The policeman looked out of his window and told me that he would tow my car if I didn't put winter tires on within two hours. Driving to the junkyard, I only put on the two winter tires on the side the police officer could see from the window.

Turns out, I was absolutely right! The cop was too lazy to get out in the snow to check my snow tires for himself. Instead, he just looked out of his window again and gave me a thumbs up. I was able to continue driving scot-free!

Just a week later, my accelerator pedal froze when the car started. Instead of immediately turning the car off again, I tried to loosen the pedal with my hand. Unfortunately, the cold engine ran too high and gave up its piston seizure, and that was it. I got 100 DM from the scrapyard for it. My next car was a red VW Golf that cost me only 2,400 DM, which lasted me for 5 years.

Between the ages of 15 and 21, I wrote around 5,000 film reviews, read at least 250 books on film, wrote reviews for Bäckerblume at the princely sum of 30 DM per article, and even managed to sell some reviews on the radio (WDR and Deutsche Welle) for 250 DM per 3-minute production. Calling myself a journalist, I got to interview Bernd Eichinger and Bo Derek. With one WDR freelance employee ID card and a fake press ID card from the screenwriters' association, I managed to go to all the cinemas and film premieres in Cologne for free. I went to the premieres of *Manta, Manta* (1991) and all the Helge Schneider comedies. I wrote around 20 screenplays and submitted applications for both film and TV funding, but only received rejection after rejection in return.

At the time, it was a requirement to complete 16 months of either military or social service. I elected to do social services, driving an ambulance and delivering groceries to the elderly. After this was complete, Frank and I finally wanted to make our first real film. We convinced a cameraman from Bayer's advertising film department to get us all the equipment and be our director of photography. In the end, we only needed about 10,000 DM in cash per our calculation, but shortly before the start, Frank had the impression that the film would ultimately just be made by me alone. It was called Wichser der Welt (The World's Wanker). I came up with the story based on my thoughts, and it was really depressing bullshit: an isolated young man fails and runs amok. The film didn't get made, and it was better that way. I only filmed part of it by myself on my VHS camera, embodying the isolation of a young man who fails and runs amok. This is a theme I would often return to in later films like *Amoklauf* (1994), *Heart of America* (2002), my *Rampage* trilogy, *Assault on Wall Street* (2013), and *Hanau* (2022).

I kept doing my sports and waited for the future. Did I have a future? Did I have a perspective to make real films?

HOLIDAYS THROUGH EUROPE

I went on a bike tour to England with my school friend Uwe Gillessen, and we rode over 100 km on the first day with our fully packed crappy bikes. The bikes weren't up to the task. We were so fed up that we sent the bikes back home via train on the third day and continued on by bus.

Once, on an Interrail tour across Europe, we started with four people: Frank, Uwe, Dietmar and me. Interrail was popular at the time. For only 400 DM, you could buy a ticket and go for free on trains all throughout Europe. Our plan was to start in Cologne, head to Madrid, and then finish over in Lisbon. To save money, we slept in tents at the beach. On day one, Frank burned himself in the sun so badly that he had to go to a hospital. The second night at the beach, a group of young locals wanted to rob us. Thanks to the help of fellow campers in Hamburg, we got out of that bad situation. I got an ulcer on my lip and could barely speak. Dietmar and I stayed in the same tent. Once, our tent pole broke and we had to sleep with the walls of the tent smushed against our faces. To be even more thrifty, we mainly ate ravioli from the can.

After one week, Frank wanted to continue alone, and Uwe wanted to go home. Nevertheless, Dietmar and I continued our trip together. On a camping ground, we met two girls, but we couldn't agree which one of us would sleep with what girl. We were sitting at the campfire, but one of the girls said she was going to her tent to sleep, expecting that one of us would follow her in. Instead, Dietmar and I wanted the girl who was still sitting at the campfire until it got so late that she went also to sleep. In the end, neither of us scored, and we both stayed virgins at the ripe old age of 20. We were total losers.

We continued our trip all the way through France, Italy and Yugoslavia, and then back over for the last leg from Paris to Cologne. On the last evening in Paris, we arrived too late, we had to sleep in front of the train station because it was locked overnight. Our train would leave very early in the morning, so I tried to sleep on my air mattress. I had my photo suitcase tucked under my arm. Suddenly, I realized a guy was pulling at it, trying to steal it out from under my arm. I crawled out of my sleeping bag and got ready to fight the thief, but he ran away. Finally, we got on our train and came home, exhausted after hundreds of hours of train rides.

A year later, Dietmar, Jens, Peter, Willms, and I drove on holiday to Jen's parent's apartment in the south of Spain. We drove over 2,200 kilometers and reached the end after about 25 hours. Dietmar drove the last eight hours and was already hallucinating. I couldn't drive because shortly before the trip, I ripped my ligaments in my left knee and was only able to walk on crutches. Dietmar and Jens were at their wits' end, but Dietmar still drove on at 170 km per hour like a maniac to stay awake, going 70 km over the speed limit.

In the end, this trip was extremely bad for all three of us because we were all frustrated, had no girlfriends, and I could only walk around on crutches. To save money, we ate the cans of food that were in the apartment, including goulash soup that had been expired for eight years! We threw loose coins from the balcony to the children in front of the house, who then rang our apartment's doorbell and asked for more money. Willms surfed out in the ocean and didn't come back as expected. Several hours later, a boat brought him back. He was only able to surf straight ahead but could never change the tail around to turn back to shore. A shell gambler fraud in a local market took 150 DM from me (100 of which was from Willms, who blindly trusted his money to me). The rare highlight in the trip happened when we were at the illegal market when the police arrived. All the dealers started running. We grabbed several tracksuits (cheap Lacoste knock-offs) from the street and ran away!

I was practically on one leg with the crutches in my hand. At night, we were so bored that we cut open melons and threw the whole pulp through the open windows into other people's houses, making a huge mess.

Frank studied Communication Sciences in Essen and wrote for the Film-Echo Magazine. I applied to local film schools (at that time, the only ones in Germany were in Berlin, Munich, and Vienna) while I worked at Bayer Leverkusen for a whole year, went to training every day, and earned 2,500 DM a month with another 1,000 DM on top of that from other activities. I taught video and football courses for the Youth Center Bunker (so named because it was a real bunker in World War II) in Leverkusen. I also gave German tutoring in a late repatriate home in Burscheid and wrote for the Wochenpost, a local newspaper. At the age of 22, I was the sports director of the newly founded radio station Radio Leverkusen, earning 1,500 DM per month. At the same time, I also started publishing book reviews and video reviews, which allowed me to get free review copies of books and movies from dozens of publishers. Over the course of 15 years, I received over 3,000 books and DVDs worth at least 30,000 DM at retail for free. Around 3 years ago, I started selling all of it on Momox and eBay, making around 5,000 euros altogether. Of course, my beautiful VHS collection was worth next to nothing.

A short time later, Frank and I came up with the idea of making a film like *The Kentucky Fried Movie* (1977), a gag compilation. The advantage of making a film this way was that you could film different actors at different times in different places, shooting it scene by scene, ultimately finishing the film over a longer period. WDR Radio did a story on us, asking local actors and crew members to help us with our film. We found our cameraman Richard Eckes and Volker Rodde, who wanted to rent us the 35mm equipment as investment. We decided to title our film *German Fried Movie,* and the budget was approximately 60,000 DM. Frank had saved 40,000

DM himself, and we wanted to find a few additional investors. After I was interviewed by WDR Radio, we received an investor letter from a guy named Boxheimer, who then brought us around four investors who invested a total of 30,000 DM.

We decided to set up our company as a GmbH, which is like an LLC in the US. To start our account, we had to pay on our company bank account 25,000 DM of share capital in cash. I had 12,500 DM from Frank in cash sitting at my house. I wanted to drive to the Burscheider Savings Bank to deposit the money. Arriving at the bank, I stood in front of the counter and couldn't find the envelope with all the cash anymore. I looked everywhere in my car, drove back home, and still couldn't find it. What the hell was happening?

The answer couldn't get any stupider! I still get angry thinking about it. What ended up happening was I put the envelope with the 12,500 DM on the roof of the car when I got in and then drove off. Halfway to the city savings bank, the envelope blew off the roof and all the money fell onto the street. What's funny is as I drove my car back home from the savings bank in a panic to check if I had left the envelope at home, I drove past the people who had just collected my money up from the street. A Dutch truck driver pocketed around 9,000 DM of the money. He was even interrogated by the police a month later, but he denied everything and wouldn't give anything back. Luckily, 2,000 DM picked up by a Volksbank employee was returned. The whole incident was in the newspaper the next day, and I was the laughingstock in our small city. Frank wanted to wring my neck. I promised Frank that I would earn all that lost money back, which I did. The crazy thing at the end of it all, it turns out I didn't need to deposit the 12,500 DM in the first place to set up our limited company. The bank only checks for the 25,000 DM sum a month after the account is opened. In the end, my bringing the money in the envelope to the bank so early was all for nothing!

MONEY

There are so many money guides and anti-money books, it almost seems like there are two parties: one who chases money all their life and the other who tries to get away from it and wants to make it clear to themselves and society that money is not important or at least not everything. Now that I am 58 years old and have had a lot of experience, I have seen a lot of poverty and a lot of wealth. It is my opinion that both sides are right and wrong. You need money. Without money, you get sick, you're dependent on others, you feel like shit, and most of the time you're not really happy. Money gives you security and self-confidence. And yet, if you only live to earn more and more money so that you can become richer and richer or buy more and more luxury goods (cars, boats, watches, houses, top of the line vacations), then you're an idiot.

Lots of people brag that they have money. I don't care. I agree with the famous quote from the founders of Aldi: "The only way to have money is not to spend it!"

If you want to make films, you're going to need money. Painters, sculptors and writers have it much easier because their calling costs almost nothing to practice. Unfortunately, film is an expensive hobby. That's why the life of a filmmaker revolves around money almost all the time, and that money is very important to the center of his life. In my case, since I took great care of my money from childhood on and was always thrifty, money never really corrupted me. This was even the case much later on when I managed millions of dollars both through my film funds, box office gross and DVD sales. For me, that money was merely numbers on an account. I never forgot that it was not my money. I had to spend it wisely for film productions by being as thrifty as possible. I always wanted to get the maximum value for a minimum capital investment. I never had the desire to spend money like the rich, nor have I ever wanted to. Neither luxury cars, bulky watches, golf, boats, or flights in private jets have ever interested me. The only luxury I treat myself to is great food and wine, but we'll get to that later.

Now we're going to discuss how Frank and I made our first feature film, *German Fried Movie*.

GERMAN FRIED MOVIE

We had our 60,000 DM together and our crew and equipment. While I was more focused on finances and the big picture, Frank was very good at the small details finding great actors, filming locations, and film gear. I wrote a lot of scenes and took care of sponsorship with product placement both in the film and on the poster. We had cars from Seat and Ford available to rent for free, food from numerous restaurants, shoes from Lloyds, clothes from Reebok, and much more. This way, I made up the 12,500 DM that had been blown away by the wind. Almost at the same time, I was filming another documentary about the University of Cologne, because that's where I was now studying. I wasn't accepted into film schools, making my visits to Munich and Vienna pointless. In Vienna, I took part in the entrance exam and wasn't accepted because I didn't have the right artistic approach. In Munich, Prof. Oswalt von Richthofen let me be a guest PA in a graduation film titled Bonnie and Clyde. I left the shoot after a day because the director seemed completely incapable, and no one had any work for me to do. The director mostly lazed about on the set talking to himself.

20 years later, my regular cameraman Mathias Neumann told me that he was filming a 2-part TV series in Turkey, and the director was completely incompetent. On one day of filming, she was sorting out small stones that were lying on the ground because they didn't work for the scene. Mathias told her that the filming location was 500 meters away, and that she was crawling around pointlessly on the ground in the parking lot. When he told me the story, I thought this might have been the same director from my time back in Munich.

I hitchhiked back from Munich in the pouring rain and managed to be driven home by someone in a Golf from Bergisch Gladbach. I enrolled in Cologne for German Literature and Language and Social Sciences. My first semester was so shitty that it inspired me to write the script *The First Semester*, which I then shot on video with the young actor Peter Kotthaus in the lead role. While I was filming my university documentary, I met my first real girlfriend, Barbara Valder, who also ended up acting in the film.

Most days, I was sitting alone in my room either typing my scripts on my typewriter or watching films. I wasn't exactly in contact with women a lot and didn't understand them either. I wanted to fuck, but I wasn't really interested in a relationship. Anger wasn't necessarily helpful because I felt that if you don't have sex or love, you'll die alone of cancer. Most of the time, I didn't talk to women, but every once in a while, I tried. At some point, it worked. A female hockey player invited me to her house over the weekend. We ended up just kissing, but a week later when my Parents were not at home, we tried to have sex. It was hard to get inside her because she was a virgin. I finally managed to do it, but she was bleeding like there was no tomorrow. In a panic, we pulled the bed linen off and threw it into the washing machine. The whole act took four minutes. When my Parents came back, of course they wanted to know why the washing machine was running. I told them my Coke bottle had spilled on the bed. We were both 20 years old, and I think she just wanted somebody to deflower her. We did it one more time, and that was it. We had nothing in common. The dam had broken, and I felt a lot better.

After a few short affairs, I met Barbara, who not only studied music and played the cello, but was also a competitive swimmer. She had to be in my short film The First Semester, which was shot in Dietmar's room at the student dormitory. Later, we shot parts of the feature film of *The First Semester* (1997) with Christian Kahrmann in this dormitory too. Dietmar invited me to a New Year's Eve party, but I drank too much. I was so drunk by 8 p.m. that I fell backwards into the buffet, collapsing the tables and spilling food all over the floor. On the way out to get the fresh air, the whole staircase was full of vomit. I lay outside on the sidewalk for an hour while Dietmar tried to calm things down. I slept 12 hours straight and was never allowed to go back to that house ever again.

We made *German Fried Movie* from 1990 to 1991. It was learning on the job day by day. We shot a few scenes on 16mm and others on 35mm, depending on what film gear we could get at the time. Agfa, Fuji, and Kodak supported us, as did the Hadeko lab in Neuss. We always shot one or two scenes in one day, and then took a break for a few weeks to prepare for the next scene. Our mothers made sandwiches, and our friends played extras for free. Richard Eckes both ran the camera and edited the film under the pseudonym Hans Wurst (Hans Sausage).

We even managed to shoot a scene in a hot-air balloon. When working on a sequence in a sports plane, I accidentally stepped on the wing while boarding the plane, leaving a hole in the wing. At that point, as head of Sports at Radio Leverkusen, I had good contacts with the air sports clubs and got everything for free. I did a bungee jump for the radio, a parachute jump, and a flight with loops in a painted biplane (the loops almost made me vomit!). It was relatively easy to get actors because they only needed to work with us for one or two days at a time.

The structure of *German Fried Movie* centered around a TV that changes from channel to channel. Throughout the film, we watch programs that make fun of movies, news, TV shows, The Iraq War, and the Gladbeck hostage drama. There were also elements of real satire in there like the Danger Seeker character committing theft in the Cologne Kaufhof, causing a ruckus an the *Manta, Manta* premiere, or doing a beer test with bums. In principle, *German Fried Movie* was a pioneer of later successful German TV shows such as *Saturday Night* (1993) or *Today's Show* (2009).

After the film was released, Frank and I were briefly employed as authors of *Saturday Night* and the *Tom Gerhardt Show*. After eight months, our film was finally finished, and we tried to get a cinema distributor. We showed the film during the film festival Berlineale in a Berlin cinema and got good reviews from Taz, Tap, and Zitty magazines. During the screening, I also met Michael Rösch, the boss of Kinostar, who was running his first cinema in Neckarsulm at the time. He invited me to come in person. Today, Michael and I have also been working in global sales for over 20 years together. Molto Menz from Filmwelt was close to closing a deal with us, but in the end but it didn't offer a contract that would have earned us any money back. Luckily, Universum Film bought the DVD rights for 25,000 DM, and then we then did the cinema distribution ourselves. Back then, it was easier to get cinemas that sometimes took a risk with small films. We ran for four weeks at Scala in Leverkusen, the Rex in Cologne, and at the Werkstattkino in Munich. Eventually, we played in over 40 cinemas throughout Germany for a week. We had five copies and rented the film out for about a year. We mostly got around 42% rental and made so about 15,000 DM back. You only learn filmmaking by making films.

The filming, post-production and exploitation of *German Fried Movie* was the best film school you could have because we had to do nearly everything ourselves.

BARSCHEL: A MURDER IN GENEVA

Our career continued after that because Universum-Film (now known as UFA) decided to support our next film project *Barschel: A Murder in Geneva* (1993) to the tune of 150,000 DM in exchange for the video rights. I already had the entire other industry upset at me because I attacked Dieter Kosslick on the TV show *B*; Kosslick was the head of Filmstiftung NRW, the largest film subsidy division in Germany. I also appeared on *Trifft* with Bettina Böttinger and repeatedly attacked the film funding. The Filmstiftung NRW gave us 50,000 DM in distribution funding for the theatrical release of *German Fried Movie* because the public pressure from the show was so great that Kosslick thought it was better for him if he calmed us down with a few marks. Nevertheless, I didn't stay calm which is why I basically got on the index over the years and almost never got subsidies for anything. I was an idiot not to kiss his ass like everybody else did. Later, Kosslick ended up running the Berlin Film Festival and ended up blocking anything I tried to get into the festival.

The Barschel case was still on everyone's lips in 1992. Uwe Barschel was a real German Minister President who was found dead in a Swiss Hotel Room 1987. Five years after he was fished dead out of the bathtub in the Beau Rivage Hotel in Geneva, Switzerland, the official cause of death was ruled a suicide. Both the Barschel family and journalists couldn't easily believe that his suicide could have been carried out alone. Too many traces suggested that Barschel wasn't alone in the hotel room. He had a wound on the back of his head. There was also a bottle of wine brought to the room which later disappeared. The toxicology report showed his BAC was 0.0%, but he had enough sleeping pills in his system to kill him three times over. It was also mysterious that no drug residue or medicine packages were found on the scene. It was clear to me someone had cleaned up the crime scene one way or another.

Nothing about the death of Barschel made sense. In my film, we showed three possible ways it played out: suicide alone, suicide with euthanasia, and murder. If you recreate the facts, as we did with actors, then you can better see whether something was possible or not. We felt Barschel's suicide being carried out alone was an impossibility. He either had someone give him euthanasia (maybe his brother, who happened to live in Geneva at the time), or he was murdered; the latter seemed more likely. It's important to note Barschel was near the end of a wire-tapping scandal involving his competitor Engholm, making him a danger to not just the CDU political party, but also a danger to Engholm himself. It turns out years later Engholm had known he was being spied on by a private eye but kept that information to himself while publicly acting like he was shocked at being spied on. As a result of his blatant lying to the public, Engholm had to step down a year later.

Actor Michael Rasmussen, who was already in our *German Fried Movie*, was perfect playing Barschel. In the film, we had a story within a story about a director who wants to convince a producer to make a film about Barschel. In retrospect, this was a mistake because it made the film too dialogue heavy. We had a little money this time around. Since we shot on 35mm, we spent 100,000 DM just for film material, lab costs and equipment. Richard Eckes was again on camera, and this time we shot most of the film all at once. We drove 12 hours in 2 cars to Geneva, filmed there without permission at the airport and in front of the original Beau Rivage hotel, then drove back after 10 hours of filming for another 12 hours because we didn't have any money for hotels. I drove my Seat Toledo, which we also got for free as a product placement, at 200 km an hour through the rain. One stretch, I even drove for a 1,200 km stretch while everyone else was sleeping in the car. By far, that was the longest and hardest day of filming of my life. Frank drove the other car by himself. In total, we went around 36 hours without sleep.

We shot the hotel interiors at the Davoy Hotel in Düsseldorf. The son of the owner, Günnewig, played on my handball team, so we got to use the room for free. The sequences at the villa, where the director spoke to the producer, we also were able to use for free thanks to Frank's family's friends. The family who normally lived in that villa was on holiday, so we had only six days to shoot. It was a real time crunch. When the family came back, they had to stay in a hotel for an extra night because we just had worked for 20 hours, and the house looked like a hippie commune. Every morning, Frank and I had driven all the way to Cologne to pick up Richard and five of the actors because they didn't have driver's licenses. From there, we drove to film in Essen, then dropped them back home in Cologne again at night, making for a total of 160 km driving every time.

Looking back on it, the concept for *Barschel: A Murder in Geneva* was wrong. The actors in the framing scenes were too over-the-top. Frank and I also got in each other's way as directors, making it clear we would never direct a film together again. On *German Fried Movie*, our collaboration worked because we shot individual scenes taking turns directing. On *Barschel: A Murder in Geneva*, this approach was a disaster.

Thanks to the help of a Munich taxi entrepreneur who invested 200,000 DM, we were able to afford a theatrical release in over 30 cinemas, but the film flopped completely and got bad reviews to boot. At least all the Barschel scenes are very exciting, and the content is far more accurate and correct than the TV film *Die Staatskanzlei* (1989) by Heinrich Breloer. He shot the government's side of the story, presenting only the suicide scenario. For this, he got all the TV awards and at least five gigs directing TV movies of the week, earning him millions. As for us, we got nothing, even if we told a more accurate version of the events that transpired. Over 20 years later, nobody in Germany believes that Barschel committed suicide, which is exactly how we portrayed it in our film way back in 1992.

As a tie-in to the film, we wrote the book *Barschel: A Murder in Geneva or How to Make A Film In Germany* about our impressions so far in the film business. I assumed my career was over. The money was all gone. No TV station bought *Barschel: A Murder in Geneva*, and the film also flopped on DVD. As a result, Universum didn't want to invest any more money in us.

My studies in Cologne, handball and boxing remained a constant in my life. I continued to earn money at Bayer, playing and teaching handball, working at Radio Leverkusen, and teaching at a business school in Cologne. My studies became easier for me because I became more and more aware of the structure of the university: It's not about really learning anything, but about completing the exams and getting the degrees. It's nonsense to schedule a bunch of seminars when you can get the certificate by simply doing a term paper, whether you're in class every day or not. I was interested in literature and read a lot, but also took courses in economics, politics and sociology. I took seminars on mass media or film theory; my term paper was on the TV series *Dallas* (1978).

After only eight semesters, I took my final exams in Psychology with German as my minor with an overall grade of 2.6. I got by on my short-term memory and botched notes. After that, I started my doctoral thesis because I suspected that getting a doctorate would help me in life. Besides, with my film career not getting off the ground, what else would I be doing?

My professor in Cologne refused to supervise me after I had already written 150 pages on TV series, so I was sent over to Professor Hickethier in Marburg who accepted me. Suddenly, I received mail from the university in Malburg that my degree from Cologne was not recognized, and I had to repeat my final exams. I thought I was hallucinating! Professor Hickethier sent me over to the Collaborative Research Center for Screen Media in Siegen where I met

Professor Schanze. In short order, he made it clear my work wasn't up to snuff and I'd have to heavily revise it.

My goal was to write an empirical paper that would for the first time quantitatively determine what series there are on TV worldwide and what common characteristics these series have. I had to spend hours in the libraries researching lists of TV channels and dictionaries. It helped, of course, that I had already seen over 15,000 films and written over 5,000 film reviews. I was a walking film encyclopedia and even won films books every time competing in the *You Know Cinema* quiz program hosted by Helmut Lange.

Professor Schanze ultimately hired me as a research assistant for over a year. I received a modest sum of 1,300 DM per month and only had to drive all the way over to Siegen once per week. I was able to work at home or at the West German State TV Library for the remainder of my studies. After over a year of hard work, I submitted my thesis which ran a colossal 880 pages. 150 pages were published under the name *The Series Genres*; the remainder of my work was more of an encyclopedia of TV series and unpublished, which is a shame because such a thing did not exist at the time.

The final requirement of getting a doctorate was a two-hour oral exam, where my grammar was also tested again. Some doctoral students only have to do a disputation where they explain their thesis, which is much easier than the rigorosum I had to do. Three professors grilled me on subjects not at all related to my studies. Thankfully, my short-term memory didn't fail me. I studied nonstop for three to four hours a day for nearly a month. On the day of the exam, I drove very early from Burscheid to Siegen so as not to be late due to a traffic jam. At 7.30 a.m., there was still no sign of anyone else at the university. I decided to go on an hour walk, which didn't help calm down my spiking adrenaline levels. The professors were late, and my exam started at 10 a.m. I was very hungry but couldn't get a bite to eat. The two hours dragged on like rubber and at the end of the day I got a cum laude, equivalent to a 2.2 grade.

After a quick snack at the cafeteria, I traveled back home to invite Jörg Gerlach (a fellow classmate who also just earned his doctorate) and my mother to eat at the restaurant Tomate. Even better, the meal was free because of my cinema advertising through them. When I told my father that I was now a doctor, he was proud of me and really meant it for the first time. I never saw him so happy ever again.

BOXING, SPORTS, HEALTH

The reason why I went into boxing was to learn how to beat people up. I hit puberty late and was still small and weak at 15 years of age. I couldn't get with girls, and I often felt helpless in situations. When I first went to the Bayer 04 Boxing Club, I was physically fit because I already practiced handball four times a week. As I soon learned, boxing is a different form of stress. After just three weeks, I did my first sparring match. Afterwards, I couldn't chew for days because my opponent hit me so hard. I made the mistake of not closing my mouth, and my sparring partner caught my lower jaw. Nevertheless, I stuck with boxing for 10 years and fought my way through.

A year later, my first sparring partner no longer had a chance against me. For years, I continued my boxing training, training with the Bundesliga and had thousands of very tough sparring matches. I sparred with people like the Tiger (Darius Michalczewski) and Felix Sturm (Adnan Catic), both of whom turned into World Champions. Only twice did someone hit my KO points (the chin and behind the ear), and I blacked out for a few seconds. Every time, I came back to reality before I was on the ground, so I caught myself in time not going down at all.

Physically, I was 174 cm and 75 kilos; this was short for my weight, but I could hit very hard. I knocked out or almost knocked out more than 50 opponents in sparring. My boxing experience didn't lead to me randomly beating people up on the street, but it made me feel better just in case. I learned to control my adrenaline so that it leads to action and not paralysis when I'm in danger. Boxing for so long helped me a lot in life because I remained calm in many situations where others might have freaked out.

Nevertheless, there was once an intense situation that would have been different without my boxing experience. I was watching a handball game in a sports hall, and my ex-coach Rolf Dicke, who was 190 cm and 95 kilos, sat behind me and tugged on my ears. I turned around and told him to stop that shit, but he didn't listen. I turned around and grabbed him by the collar, pulling him up the stairs into the exit corridor while other spectators looked on in surprise. He wanted to free himself and make it look like that he was in control, but he was not. Instead, we tore the fire extinguisher from the wall as we were fighting. We both fell through the glass door out of the hall onto the ground. He said I should stop, but I was on top of him where I could easily have punched his face in. Instead, I just told him to stop humiliating me once and for all, otherwise I would send him straight to the hospital. What you really learn in boxing, in addition to discipline and stamina, is how to take a punch.

Once, a Kurdish man broke my C6 vertebrae while doing a neck muscle exercise. My head jerked downwards, and you could hear it cracking. For months, I dragged myself around with a numb arm until I couldn't walk anymore. Eventually, the disc was removed by a neurosurgeon and replaced by titanium. I had to make a choice whether to have a piece of the hip bone or a titanium disc inserted. I took titanium because otherwise it would have been two separate operations. In retrospect, this was a mistake because to this day I have rejection reactions and get regular headaches.

After I stopped playing handball and boxing regularly, I went jogging every day. When I turned 45, I got arthritis of the hip, which made jogging harder. I still played rounds of tennis from time to time, but I could hardly walk the next day. Longer hikes, which I used to do regularly, were no longer possible. Of course, these were also long-term consequences of handball; I had meniscus and cruciate ligament damage in my left knee. When I turned 57, I finally replaced my hip; since then, the pain has been gone. I can do long walks, bike rides, swimming, and weight training instead of running, tennis, squash, and other sports I used to enjoy.

My daily routine looks like this: 15-25 minutes on the bike plus 50 push-ups, 30 pull-ups, and a few other exercises for the abdominal muscles. I don't do it because I enjoy it, but because my father had his first heart attack when he was 49, and I'm now 58. I want to continue to feel fit and healthy. I've never smoked or taken any drugs. I make sure I get enough sleep, exercise, and good food. Alcohol in the form of red wine (although sometimes I partake a beer with a shot of grappa) is my only sin; even then, I try to stay alcohol-free three days a week. The famous saying "Without health, everything is nothing!" is true, and you should behave accordingly. I already have enough stress in my life that I don't have to worry about cigarettes, drugs, or sleep deprivation. I've seen many crew members and actors take drugs over the years and can only say that I have absolutely zero interest in drugs myself.

AMOKLAUF

Frank and I didn't know what to do next after *German Fried Movie* and *Barschel Mord In Genf*. We still had about 40,000 DM left in our bank account. Frank agreed that I could make a film with it. Since I assumed that it was to be my final film, I wanted to say goodbye with a dark and powerful message. *Amoklauf* was shot with a treatment consisting of only one page of text with almost no dialogue. Michael Rasmussen, an actor we used in *Barschel Mord In Genf*, played the lead role of a nihilist serial killer. We only show his world and not that of the police squad investigating him. He says life is pointless, and the only goal we have is death. The last eight minutes of the film is a slow-motion amok run, ending with the shooter surviving walking off into the light. I was very satisfied with the film. It was only shown in five cinemas and was distributed on VHS by Jelinski-Buttgereit and later on a horror DVD label. *Amoklauf* also appeared in competition at the Max Ophüls Festival to the horror of all arthouse journalists.

It was time for me to get a "real job", so I applied to TV and production companies. I worked as a teacher at a business school, at the radio, at the newspaper, in a repatriate home, and at a Mannesmann steel factory. I also worked as an extra and PA for *Der 7. Sinn* and at the WDR school of television. Other jobs at this time included working at the same chemical plant Bayer AG in Leverkusen where my father also worked for 45 years and working in construction with Frank at his father's company. For additional income, I delivered mail to the members of the sports club, mowed my grandma's lawn every week for 10 years, and even played some handball.

I lost my job at Radioleverkusen as sports director as a new editor-in-chief took over and kicked out one employee after the other. He was a mega asshole, and I decided to teach him a lesson when I slashed his car tires and screamed at him over the phone every night for weeks. Once he yelled back, but he had no idea who was calling, and I felt he was scared. I then stopped because I was afraid that the police would eventually trace the phone line back to me. My time working in radio was great because we could actually do whatever we wanted, and I had a great crew together with Klaus Schenkmann and Peter Liebertz. We were everywhere, and Leverkusen was a great sports city full of Bundesliga handball, volleyball, basketball, football, motoball, and boxing.

THE FIRST SEMESTER

When the dead German ex-chancellor Helmut Kohl didn't announce the secret donors for his party because he had given his word of honor not to reveal them, he was torn apart by the entire press and the other politicians. I hate Helmut Kohl, but with this action he earned my respect. I, too, keep my word. When I promise something, I stick to it. To be clear, it was against the law that he took that money for his party, and he shouldn't have accepted it. Nevertheless, he accepted it and gave his word, otherwise they wouldn't have given him any money. If he had broken his word just because he was threatened with jail, then in my eyes he would have been a little lousy wanker. The people who criticized Kohl for that are the typical flags in the wind who have a big mouth as long as everything is going well. In the end, they always abandon their friends in order to protect themselves.

I applied to at least 25 production companies and TV channels, but only received rejections. Later, at a party in Cologne, I met Detlev Brosztek from the Dortmund company Westcom. He was well known for the Sat 1 Regional Report News and now wanted to get into the fiction business. He loved my film *German Fried Movie* and wanted to work with me in Dortmund as a writer and producer. I met his partners Peter Pohl and Georg Hirschberg, who now produces the ZDF Today Show. They hired me for 60,000 DM a year.

My idea was to make my student film *The First Semester* better and bigger. I hoped Westcom could push that production forward. I told them I was on the blacklist of the Film Subsidies, but that the power of Westcom was even greater. We actually received 1 million DM in funding from them and made the film. I raised another million from two private investors. We kept the project going even though I ended up leaving Westcom after just their months because

Taunus Film in Wiesbaden hired me as assistant to Prof. Wolfgang Grass, their Managing Director.

Taunus Film was beautifully located in Wiesbaden "unter den Eichen" and had studios, a lab, and post-production facilities. They were also co-owned by Public TV. For the first time, I moved away from my home and my girlfriend Barbara. Every Friday, I drove back home to Cologne. Every Sunday, I returned back to Wiesbaden, a 360 km roundtrip.

Dietmar moved to Nürnberg and worked for Adidas in the marketing department. Frank worked for the film journal Film Echo, and my brother worked for the TV channels Vox and WDR. He was a TV journalist who did reports for *Voxtours* and *Sportschau*. Jens Peter worked in sales for the OCE printer company. He stayed there all his life, but they were acquired by Canon years later. Dietmar would switch from one employer to another, such as jumping from Chupa Chups to Bat (Lucky Strike). Every time he did so, he got a higher salary. Willms never made those big jumps in salary because he stayed with one company.

In Wiesbaden, I got paid more money than ever before, making 110,000 DM per year right away. I rented a nice apartment very close to the studio so I could walk to work. I met the Wiesbaden cinema owner Ewert and got an annual ticket. Most days I would eat spaghetti or kebabs, go jogging every day, and then go to the cinema or watch TV. I didn't really meet any new friends for the first year, until I met a Citibank employee Esther Jacobi and her boyfriend Christoph. Both of them are still my friends today, even though they later moved to New York for several years and now live in Bavaria.

Grass was someone who grew up rich. He was gay but didn't admit it. He realized very quickly that I was very direct and rather blunt. He also recognized that I'm not a good assistant, so he made me a producer and hired someone else as an assistant.

His deputy, Mr. Richter, initially liked me but this changed later on when I criticized him very hard in public. He had no clue on how to produce a film but was working there for political reasons because the state had an interest in Taunus Film. Richter was a hunter and ex-mayor of Taunusstein and joined for political reasons years ago. He had no idea about the media and was thoroughly corrupt, like so many people I got to know during my time there. I told him to his face that he was full of hot air.

The First Semester feature got also UIP (Universal) as a distributor and Vox as a TV partner, earning around 250,000 DM profits for Taunus Film. Leo Kirch, the most powerful German media boss who essentially created private TV in Germany, almost bought the TV rights to *The First Semester*. Interested, I drove to Munich to close the deal. However, their bid was lower than the 300,000 DM Vox was offering. I turned down Kirch, which pissed him off so much he personally called Grass to complain. Grass told me that Kirch had been annoyed and that this wasn't a good idea for future business, but I stayed with Vox. To date, more of my films have been shown on the RTL Group channels than Pro7 or Sat1, the latter of which were Kirch channels who changed ownership over the last 20 years various times. Nowadays, the heirs from Sergio Berlusconi (the Italian media baron and premier minister) own the majority of the channels. Only my film *Alone in the Dark* was shown on Pro7 because TeleMünchen bought the German rights and had a deal with them.

I was able to go back to Cologne for almost 2 months to shoot The First Semester with a budget of around 2 million DM, and I was very happy about that. We shot at my old university in Cologne, which was a great feeling. We had a strong Germany comedy cast with actors like Christian Kahrmann, Tana Schanzara, Radost Bokel, Willi Thomcyk, Wichard von Roell, Hilmi Sözer and Guildo Horn. The filming went well, but what was not as good was when Detlev Brosztek suffered a nervous breakdown on the first day of filming and was admitted into a hospital. It later came out that he had an overdose, but, in the end, I didn't really need him.

So, I shot the film completely by myself as producer, director and writer. I earned great money for working all these roles on the set and continued to receive my Taunus Film salary on top of it. We also got product placement deals for the film from Pizza Hut, Lloyds Shoes, Boss Suits, and Reebok.

Since I was always good with money (except when I left it on the roof of my car), this film was the start of my solid finances. I started to speculate on the stock market, which was unfortunately a mistake because every time I profited, I proceeded to lose it again. Over the years, I've been up. Until recent years, I have always earned more with bonds than with stocks. Every year, I either lost up to 10% of my savings or gained back between 3 to 12% at most. My Pan-Am shares were completely worthless, one Daewoo bond was written off worthless, and the first Commerzbank's capital cut from 260 DM down to 20 DM cost me 80%. Later, I trusted my investments more to bankers, which was a good move.

The editing of the film then took place again in Wiesbaden. We cut it on a 35mm Steenbeck table, which took a very long time. The film was mixed at Herold Studios in Frankfurt. We made a soundtrack deal with Edel Music, which let us have Scooter and The Fugees on the album. At the first screening for Paul Steinschulte, the managing director at UIP, he proclaimed, "We won't take the film, and we won't bring it to the cinema!".

This came as a complete shock. I didn't think the film was a hit either, but in the days *of Manta, Manta* where German comedies were big hits, I thought we'd do well enough with the right amount of advertising. We did a new sound mix and recut the film, but Steinschulte still hated it. We were only released in 50 cinemas. Our promotional tour with the actors and me only was in East Germany, so the film flopped. Good thing I still had my job at Taunus Film where I diligently brought in filmmakers that used our post-production facilities.

We founded Taunus Film International with me as the managing director. As a perk, I got a company credit card, which I used for gas and restaurants. I also got my very own secretary. They put me in a penthouse office, which unfortunately became a sauna in the summer due to its large glass windows. As part of the job, I also traveled to more events to interest directors and producers in our services. My first new car was a Hyundai Lantra, which was inexpensive but could reach up to 200 km per hour if needed; this made it quite convenient for my weekend trips to Cologne.

Frank Schleinstein wanted us to produce his directorial feature debut, *The Mystery Of Cormoran Island* (1997), which was financed primarily through funding and TV broadcasters like ORB and the NDR. Both the budget discussions with the NDR production manager and the location and dramaturgy discussions with the editor Arno Alexander were exhausting because I was in no way interested in the film. I only agreed to the whole thing because I could make money with it. Filming took place in Mecklenburg-Vorpommern, and the crew was almost exclusively Ossis, who were former East Germans until the fall of the Berlin Wall.

My production manager called me after two days of filming and told me the lighting technicians hadn't come because it was a Saturday. Of course, you can also film on Saturdays and the lighting technicians knew that. There was no reason to suspect a holiday on the second day of filming. I fired all the electricians and brought in a new crew from Frankfurt to replace them. The film was completed on budget in the end. I wasn't once on location because I didn't feel like driving for seven hours. The lighting technicians sued us and won in the labor court, so everyone got an extra five days of pay. This is, of course, a total joke, but that's how it ended up. The director Frank Schleinstein was only allowed to make the film because his wife was an editor at the ORB, which is how it often is in the film industry with its complete corruption and vitamin B economy.

Christa Gerlach and Achim Appel were more successful colleagues than him. Gerlach, the ex-wife of the Kirch consultant and Ex Sat1 editor-in-chief Peter Gerlach, landed major contracts for Taunus Film such as *Kurklinik Rosenau* (1996) or *Natalie-Endstation Babystrich* (1994) at SAT1. The problem was, she was not a great producer. If she got 20 million DM for a TV series, she never made for than 400,000 profit off of it. Co-CEO Richter knew that if I would have produced this, we would made 4 million DM in profits every season. Nevertheless, Gerlach insisted on keeping control.

Achim Appel did the local news and ran a Business TV Channel for the Deutsche Bank, which made him several million DM in profits per year. Appel and Neata later left Taunus Film in order to pocket the money themselves. Today, he runs Kinowelt TV. So much in German TV runs on pure nepotism. No one gets a series order because they have a good idea. Orders are only available to companies that belong directly or indirectly to the broadcasters or to companies with quasi-friendly relationships with the decision-makers of the broadcasters. That's also the reason why so much shit is produced for the broadcasters. It's not a competition for the best ideas, but simply pure corruption through and through. If broadcaster bosses say that there are no quotas their producers have to meet, then they are lying.

All the scandals surrounding Jurgan from the ARD or Degeto and Heintze from the NRD are just the tip of the iceberg and they are all true. In Germany, around 100 producers shared around 2 billion euros per year amongst themselves, which the broadcasters spend on orders. I personally took care of the TV company TV 2000, which had fixed contracts with ARD and ZDF. *White And Blue Stories, Holidays From Allday*, and *Urlaub Vom Alltag* were typical of the productions we aired. Unfortunately, the owners often didn't have the ability to carry out financially successful productions, so the debts at Taunus Film were related to office rent and post-production services. It's just often the case that producers in

Germany, which have contacts and good ideas in terms of funding, are absolute complete failures on the set and simply cannot manage to keep anything on budget.

Mr. Richter convinced Mr. Grass that I should produce an episode of the music show *Urlaub Vom Alltag* for TV2000 with the same crew that would always do the same shit. The director was also the cameraman; and he was very good as both. Filming took place on the Canary Islands in Spain and the SWR editor Hirschmann came along with his wife. They enjoyed a nice holiday in a 5-star hotel at the broadcaster's expense. The SWR and MDR paid a total of around 750,000 DM for a 90-minute program; in the end, it was their show. Folk music singers such as Karel Gott and Kristina Bach, which were all very nice, sang their songs in the harbor or on the beach or in a restaurant in that holiday paradise. It couldn't have been easier. I convinced the singers' managers that we only pay for their flight and hotel accommodation because the show was advertising for them. We got the flights (TUI) and hotels (RIO) for free thanks to product placement in the film. Richter called me, and I had to hand over several thousand DM to Hirschmann, a clear bribery. Nevertheless, I made that production for 550,000 DM, which made Taunus Film a 200,000 DM profit and netted me a 20,000 DM bonus.

I explained to Grass that if I produced something like *Kurklinik Rosenau*, it would earn at least 5 million DM in profits. Sadly, this was Mrs. Gerlach's show, and she didn't want to use me as producer. The time between 1995 and 1998 went by very fast. I was no longer a director, but just a producer, and barely one at that. I shot a few commercials, even a short film for Porsche, a Pall Mall spot in NY, and two animation spots for Lucky Strike. We shot Pall Mall in NY, but the ad-agency guys from Grey were absolute idiots. We had to shoot about 25 scenes with young people who were only visible for 3 seconds each, which means each shot would last 2 seconds. The shots were of two guys high fiving each other or smiling, that kind of shit. We cast everyone and had 3 days of filming at 25 locations, so we didn't have a lot of time. After I shot the first scene three times, I said, "All right, onto the next shot!" One of Grey's bitches flipped out completely, shouting, "That's not how it works... You'll have to offer me something else!" I looked at her and asked, "What? Is there a spaceship landing in the background?" Grey wanted to get me fired and called Germany to complain, but the head of marketing of BAT told her to shut the fuck up. The finished clip was great.

At that time, agencies still had high budgets for commercials, and I earned a lot of money from them. I always had such projects run through my company Bolu Film, which now belonged to me alone. I was able to use Taunus Film for post-production. My long-distance relationship with Barbara eventually ended, but we remain good friends to this day.

I found a new girlfriend in Christine Öhrling. She was from Jena and studied in Mainz, working as an intern for one of our tenants. I had an invitation to a film premiere in Frankfurt and invited her. We got closer, but she had a boyfriend who she wanted to leave. I bought an attic apartment in Mainz because it was cheaper than in Wiesbaden, and we moved in together after dating for a year-and-a-half.

ANIMAL WELFARE

At this time, I also started going for walks with dogs over at the Mainz Animal Shelter. Every free minute I could, I took the dogs out. Since I grew up with dogs, I wasn't afraid of them at all, not even Rottweilers or Pitbulls. My Parents first had a Münsterländer named Bodo, who once almost bit off my ear and eventually died of old age at 13. He bit at least 30 people. One guy got attacked driving by on his moped and fell off! My Parents had to pay him 5,000 DM to make up for it.

After Bodo died, we got the wolfhound Bubu. My brother always went to the breeders in Solingen and worked there, so they gave him Bubu (an 80 kilo chunker) for free. Large purebred dogs don't live long, and she had kidney failure at only seven years of age. I took her to the vet and had her put to sleep. She could barely walk. One time, I had to carry all 80 kilos of her home from the forest. It was clear her time with us was over. Afterwards, I went to a handball game, played, and drove home, crying the whole way.

Our next dogs were Vizlas puppies named Bessy and Lena. They were sisters but were totally different sizes. Bessy was a killer when it came to rabbits and birds. Lena was sometimes aggressive towards other dogs. Both were very nice overall compared to old Bodo. When they both died at the age of 13, my Parents didn't want any more dogs, which I felt was a big mistake. Dogs keep you active because you must take them on walks through harsh winds or bad weather whether you want to or not.

I always had problems with the animal shelter because I let the dogs go off the leash when I took them on walks. In my opinion, dogs have to get a good run in. If they weren't aggressive, and I was in the forest with them, I saw no reason not to let them off leash. Most of the time, I jogged alongside them. Once, when I was walked a German Wirehaired Pointer, the dog darted off. I ran after him as he ran over a hill. As I reached the top, I could see him on top of a sheep mauling it to death. The shepherd wanted 60 marks, but he let me go in the end because I didn't have any money on me.

Another time, there was a black shepherd dog named Laura. She was only four months old in her cage freshly castrated. I took her for a walk and adopted her shortly thereafter. Christine was thrilled. It turns out Laura was dropped off at the shelter by a young mother because she had "too much work" to take care of. This is typical of new dog owners; they don't realize all the work it takes to raise a dog properly.

At first, Laura playfully pinched us in the arm, giving us little bruises from her pointy teeth. Once, she got me really bad, and I hit her ass with one big slap. She turned around a full 360 degrees and ran around the apartment barking in disbelief. She couldn't believe that I had hit her! After that, she never bit us again. She was always by my side as I filmed all over the world from Romania to Canada. She died in 2014 when she was over 15, dropping down dead of a heart attack in front of my house in Vancouver. It was a perfect death for a perfect dog.

When I shot BloodRayne in Bucharest, I had Laura with me. When we got to Mediapro Studio, Laura hopped right out of the car. Straight away, a horde of wild dogs ran after her. Laura ran off with the dogs, and I ran right after her. I was scared that the dogs would attack her. Laura hid behind a stage at the film studio while I scared the wild dogs off. Every day, I jogged with her in a small forest. On the very first day, we ran into another horde of dogs that were very aggressive. There were at least 50 wild dogs in front of us, and Laura stood between my legs in fear. I yelled at the dogs to run away and walked slowly through the pack. They let us go.

The next day, I took 10 kilos of dog food with me, and all the wild dogs were excited. Three days later, I had 20 dogs that went jogging with Laura and me on a regular basis. I had to buy 20 kilos of dog food every day just to feed everyone! Every evening, I also took dog food with him, stopping at various places to feed the wild dogs that would come by.

While we were scouting for locations, I found a puppy in the dirt and took him with me, warming him under my sweater. He was covered in fleas. We drove him to the vet where he was vaccinated and deloused. I called him Fritz, and he screamed like a baby. I could barely sleep, and of course, had to work long hours shooting *Bloodrayne*. I got our costume designer Carla to adopt Fritz and threw in some extra money to help with the dog food. Years later, Fritz had grown into a big, happy dog.

There was another young dog hanging around the studio that my friend Will Sanderson wanted him all to himself, although it was clear he never took care of a dog himself before. We named the dog Daisy, and I made a bed for her in my office so that she could sleep inside at night. But every morning when I arrived, she was outside again. The security guards had thrown her out of my office every night. I told the studio staff that I wasn't joking around. I didn't want Daisy to sleep outside. The next day, Daisy was outside again limping. The security guy had kicked her out once again. I went to the head of the studio and told him that I would stop shooting *Bloodrayne* if Daisy wasn't in my office. That worked! Daisy was happy.

A little later, I took her with me to my hotel, and she peed in the elevator. I told her, "No!", and she was miraculously potty trained on the spot. Street dogs are clever. She then slept in the hotel room. She always slept on my pile of dirty laundry. She lived with Laura and died when she was 14 years old, only 2 years after Laura died. Another time, I caught an extra kicking a street dog. I ran up, threw him on the ground, and fired him on the spot.

All her life, Daisy was jealous of food. She would bite other dogs who came near her when she was eating and terrorized Laura over and over. Nobody could ever take food away from her without getting bitten. Because of Bodo, I know what a real bite is. Thankfully, Daisy's bites didn't break the skin like Bodo's.

After I watched the documentary *Earthlings* (2005), which shows people killing and torturing animals, I showed the film in Vancouver together with PETA and SPCA. I later used film from PETA in the opening credits for my film *Seed*. I offered to distribute *Earthlings* worldwide for the director Shaun Monsoon, but his producers weren't interested. This is still a big mystery to me. At the screening in Vancouver, there were many questions from the audience.

They recommended donating money to their organization and becoming vegetarian. I felt this was not enough, and that there must be political rules in place to better protect animals. There simply must not be any more battery breeding, factory farming, and senseless animal testing. Things like this must be banned! I called on all viewers if they saw animal cruelty, to immediately beat up the animal torturer. They are supposed to break into animal testing centers and free the animals and shoot a bullet in the head of every circus director who beats his animals. When it comes to animal cruelty, I get past diplomacy. Of course, the employee of the animal protection association wasn't particularly enthusiastic about my approach.

From 1998 to 1999, Taunus Film was up for sale. They wanted to keep the real estate property but sell Taunus Film Production. It was clear to all insiders that the calculations didn't really work out because the rental income from the production companies that were on our premises (such as Odeon Film, who made *Ein Fall für zwei*) , and their own rent-free living were the core of Taunus' survival. In other words, if Taunus Film had to pay rent in the future and could no longer keep their rental income, then at least 40% of their workforce would have to be laid off. At this point, the New Market Stock Exchange was introduced, which allowed many medium-sized companies to go on the stock exchange. Small companies were pumped up and put on the stock exchange at high prices. The performance of the companies was mostly bad, and the business models were not actually improved just because 50 or 100 million were flushed into their coffers through an IPO. The extreme example was EMTV, which was traded almost as high as the Walt Disney group.

The new company Cinemedia was founded and bought almost all of the film labs in Germany. It was looking for further candidates to take over in order to increase sales through acquisitions. Taunus Film made around 60 million DM in sales per year, and therefore Cinemedia was interested in acquiring it. interesting for Cinemedia. There was a meeting at Taunus Film with Holger Heims, the managing director of Cinemedia. He laid out his plans, which centered around buying Hollywood films. I stood up and protested this idea, saying, "We already have the top post-production companies. Why should we buy films when we can also produce films ourselves and increase our sales with them?" There was applause because the 250 people in the hall were working technical positions.

Around this same time, Cinemedia bought films like Mel Gibson's *What Women Want* (2000), which was actually very successful unlike the other six films they bought. When their purchase of Taunus Film went through, I was in Spain producing *Holiday From Everyday*, and I wasn't offered any shares. When I was back, I was told that Richter, Grass, Gerlach and Appel each received 2,000 shares as a gift and sold them for 130 DM each on the day of issue. I went to Grass in anger because it was actually a mistake that I didn't get anything. As a direct response, I decided to use the Taunus Film credit card more. Why eat out for 20 euros when you can eat out for 100 euros? That was also the time when I was slowly developing my love for good food and wine. Meals always taste better when you don't pay for them yourself. At this point, I was already very heavily involved in the Erste Boll Kino Beteiligungs Gmbh & Co. KG., the company that ultimately would make my first American film *Sanctimony* (2000).

FILM, MUSIC, AND LITERATURE

I've seen at least 20,000 films and written around 6,000 mini film reviews. I've seen everything from classics to porn, from *Battleship Potemkin* (1925) to *Greed* (1924), from *The Man Who Shot Liberty Valance* to *Iron Man* (2008). I have loved sitting in the movie theater since I was six years old. Whether it's *Spartacus* (1960), *Once Upon A Time In The West* (1968), *Jaws* (1975), or *Apocalypse Now* (1979), I've seen them all in the cinema. This initial enthusiasm for movies is what led to me wanting to make my own films. I started writing screenplays when I was 13 years old; usually, they were 30 to 50 pages in length. I read everything I could get my hands on about film, directors, actors, and genres.

Often, I'd go to the UFA Palace in Cologne at noon with my sandwiches and a bottle of water. After my movie was done, I secretly snuck into a different movie. I'd often have a marathon of six films until the theater closed, all while paying for a single ticket. Later, I watched films more on DVDs at home. Today, I don't go to the theater much anymore and tend to watch everything on Netflix or VOD.

In the past 20 years, I didn't love a lot of new films, but there are exceptions like *There Will Be Blood* (2007), *Map To The Stars* (2014), and *The Wolf Of Wall Street* (2013). Of course, I grew up very much with genre films. Watching horror films like *Friday the 13th* proved to be tests of courage. John Carpenter is a director I liked very much (*Escape From New York* (1981), *The Thing* (1982), *The Fog* (1980)). George A. Romero's *Dawn Of The Dead* (1978) made a very strong impression on me.

At the same time, I also found arthouse films by Truffaut, Godard and Bergmann to be of great interest. 1970s classics like *Jaws*, *The Godfather* (1972), and *Taxi Driver* (1976) are still my favorite films today. Of course, I also watched the Star Wars and Star Trek films, but to this day I'm not a big fan of the so-called event films despite my film production company being named Event Film. All of the Marvel and DC films based off the comic books are well made, but I'm less and less interested in them with each new entry. More recent blockbusters like *The Hunger Games* (2012), *The Hobbit: An Unexpected Journey* (2012), and *Captain America: The First Avenger* (2011) I only caught at home on VOD. Even then, I mostly fast-forward through them because the plots are so predictable.

Over the years, I've become more and more of a fan of documentaries and TV series. Both *Breaking Bad* and *House Of Cards* were 10 times better than any movie I've seen in the last 10 years. Some of my favorite directors include John Ford, Alfred Hitchcock, William Wyler, John Huston, Orson Welles, Stanley Kubrick, and Martin Scorsese. Not every film of theirs is great, but overall their work is quite good.

Many new directors are executing a corporate vision and are no longer true filmmakers. The studios promote young CGI talent who film what can be seen in the script and on the storyboards. They all don't have their own style, voice, or opinion. Many art-house films have no bite and are non-political, unimportant films that have a cast and look good. It costs $50 million to bring a major film into US cinemas, so each one is financially risky. Nowadays, the studios only make 10-14 films a year. Out of these, 80% are high concept films (cartoons, comic book adaptations, etc.) and 20% are comedies or dramas that are supposed to compete for the Oscars. Everything is predictable and boring. That's why you have to be so happy when, after many years of mediocrity, Scorsese finally makes another good film with *The Wolf Of Wall Street*. I had almost written him off, but luckily, he really went back to his *Goodfellas* (1990) roots with the film. That's why I'm happy about every new Tarantino film and loved *Django Unchained* (2012).

When I'm asked about my favorite film, I usually say *Apocalypse Now*, but it can't be one film alone. Other favorites include *Once Upon A Time In The West, Once Upon A Time In America* (1984), *Citizen Kane* (1941), *El Dorado, Rio Bravo,* and *Rio Grande* (1950).

As a child, I collected Star Trek cards and all the Donald Duck comics. I was a big fan of Asterix, Lucky Luke, and Lieutenant Blueberry. *MAD Magazine* was another one I enjoyed for a decade. Three years ago, I sold my entire comic collection. I've concluded it's ultimately pure nonsense to collect thousands of DVDs, books, or stamps; it's all a waste of space and money. In addition to film books, I also read novels and nonfiction books. Through my literature studies in Cologne, I was exposed to writers such as Thomas Mann, Arthur Schnitzler and Thomas Bernhard. I had a phase for about 5 years where I submerged myself in world literature and read 250 of the real classics. I don't think anyone at school should be required to read *Buddenbrooks* by Thomas Mann because at that age, you're too young to read something like that. The most interesting thing to me was learning why a writer wrote something and to dig into under what circumstances a writer wrote his work. This makes boring books look quite interesting. For example, Thomas Bernhard was a very dark and cynical writer who never got married or had friends and died kind of young when he was 60 years old. If you know his childhood story from World War II, this all makes sense. He lost his entire family and spent years in a sanitarium due to complications from open tuberculosis. It is not surprising that after these years the spoiled post-war generation seemed to him like a hypocritical, arrogant band of snots.

For the last 15 years, I have read almost only non-fiction books, biographies, and articles in political magazines. I'm not so much into lengthy fictional books anymore. Of course, I read scripts, contracts and emails all day. I answer all my emails every day, so that I can start the next day fresh.

As for music, I listen to everything from pop to heavy metal and classical. I love Bruce Springsteen, Billy Joel, Yes, Thin Lizzy, Supertramp and many more! I was never so much into Kiss, AC/DC, The Rolling Stones, or The Beatles despite their popularity. I love Rammstein more for their lyrics than their music. While filming the *In the Name of the King: The Last Mission* (2014) in Sofia, Bulgaria, I met Rammstein's lead singer, Til Lindemann. I think one of my actors was his friend who partied with him a lot. He was very reserved and completely different than on stage. Later, I expected to meet him again for dinner in Berlin, but he didn't come or reply to my emails anymore. Total bullshit as usual!

I think Richard Strauss's *Tod Und Verklärung* is the best classical symphony ever written. I even used the final 10 minutes of it for *Amoklauf*.

When I wrote scripts, I often would listen to instrumental music like Bach's *Brandenburgische Orgelkonzerte* or Mike Oldfield's *Tubular Bells* and *Ommadawn*. I wrote both on a typewriter and in my diary. In 2023, I unpacked all 880 pages, scanned them in the computer, and edited them for my book *Tabula Rasa*; it documents my childhood and youth up until my time at Taunus Film great detail. Although writing was something I did every day in my youth, for the past 15 years, it's been more difficult to concentrate and focus.

SANCTIMONY

During my time at Taunus Film from 1994 to 2000, I didn't direct any features. I earned a lot of money but didn't love my job. at Taunus Film. After my film *The First Semester* flopped, nobody asked me to direct a film for them. My own film ideas were more akin to American genre cinema.

I noticed that there were more and more film funds in Germany raising money from German investors which were then used it to finance international films. The investors were able to deduct 100% of their film investments from taxes for the same year. Let's say a dentist has an annual income of 200,000 euros and he normally pays 100,000 euros in taxes. If he invested the 200,000 euros into a film fund instead, he would have to pay no taxes. In the end, of course, this is a tax dodge because the proceeds of the films must themselves be taxed. In this example, the dentist would only invest 200k if he felt he could get his entire investment back again.

Investing in film funds in Germany was once a good investment for those in higher tax brackets or for those with a large severance payment as long as the film earned more than its budget. These funds have often been released by banks or their subsidiaries as leasing models. The investor gets financed by the bank with up to 80% of the investment as a loan. So, an investor who kicks in 100k actually only pays 20k of it himself but saves 50k in taxes directly. The 80% provided as a loan gets repaid with proceeds of the film. Some of the more lucrative funds even guaranteed proceeds of 30 to 130% of the amount initially investment. Who wouldn't invest in that?

These German film markets lasted from 1990 to 1999, and they were buzzing with a subscription volume of over 3 billion euros per year. Helaba (Hessische Landesbank) had bought 10% of Taunus

Film at this point. Their subsidiary was Hannover Leasing over in Munich, so I got in contact with them. Hannover Leasing were prepared to give me a term sheet in which they would give me 20 million DM for an American film as long as I could secure 2 well-known actors and a 60% distribution guarantee, which guaranteed proceeds from an American distributor!

With this term sheet, I was able to fly to Los Angeles on Taunus Film's dime. Germans were very popular there because the film funds were booming, and every Hollywood producer wanted some of that German money. I met several distributors. Even Duncan Clark, President of Sony/Columbia Films, gave me an hour of his time. Nobody wanted to be tied down to the 60% return guarantee.

I wanted to make my own film with the title *The End Of The Second Millennium*. It was a serial killer thriller later released as my first American film under the title *Sanctimony*. The script, direction, and production were all to be done by me. Hollywood was used to just getting money from the German funds, but such funds had no input into the Hollywood films. In my case, I wanted to keep creative control. Therefore, the Hollywood studios didn't have to pay for the budget. They would only get a feature film for free for distribution, but they had to return it to me even if the film was a flop earning only 60% of its budget. To most, this was a risky proposal. I never gave up and tried to convince various companies.

One evening, I was sitting at the Italian restaurant Il Sole on Sunset Boulevard. Mickey Rourke came in alone with his little dog in tow. The dog was eating carpaccio from the same plate as him. I went over to his table, introduced myself as a German filmmaker who had a script for a film where he could play a serial killer or a policeman, whichever part he wanted. He asked me about the script, and I had it in my car, but it was parked 1 km away. I ran off and got it for him. I was awoken at 4 a.m. with a call from Mickey. He said he wanted to play the cop and talked about scenes that weren't even in the script. He arranged to meet me at Is Sole again for dinner the next evening at 7 p.m. sharp.

I met him at the restaurant the next time and surprised him with a Dutch TV team who gave him a life achievement award right there in the restaurant. We had a nice dinner but didn't talk at all about my script. Once again, we agreed to meet again the next day at 7 p.m.! By this time, I had memorized the whole menu. He came in with his lawyer, and they wanted $1 million for him to play the part of the cop. At this point, Mickey's career was in the toilet; I had heard that he was worth, at most, only $300,000, which I offered him. Rourke and his lawyer got up and left. I was left with three plates full of food and the check.

I had barely finished all of the food (I hate to waste it!) when I noticed Jean Claude van Damme on the sidewalk waiting for his car. I didn't hesitate for a second and ran over to pitch him the project. He agreed to meet at 9 a.m. the next morning at the Beverly Hills Hotel. Van Damme was more successful than Mickey Rourke's at that point, but he wasn't at his peak either. The next morning, I drove to the Beverly Hills Hotel, parked for $20 (an outrageous price in the year 2000; these days, it would cost $100), and went into the restaurant. I couldn't find him, so I waited outside the main entrance. Helen Hunt sat near me leaning up against the wall. I only noticed it was her after she already was picked up. After a 20-minute wait, a car pulled up to me. The driver asked if I was waiting for Van Damme.

We drove to the villa of the former Paramount boss and Oscar winner Bob Evans (*The Godfather, Love Story* (1970), *Chinatown* (1974)). Both Van Damme and Evans were already lounging between the tennis court and the pool house. I pitched my project to both of them who were clad only in bathrobes. Evans said to Van Damme, "Well, I have a good feeling about this crazy German.!" Van Damme insisted I finance his film *Replicant* (2001) instead, which was of no interest to me. I told him he could work with me on my film, or not work with me at all. In short order, they walked me back to my car.

Nevertheless, Jürgen Prochnow (*Das Boot* (1981)) and Eric Roberts (*Runaway Train* (1985)) managed to get on board through private channels. Avi Lerner from Nu Image gave me the 60% guarantee without even reading the script. Avi was one of the producers who was flooded with German money and became a top producer as a result (*The Expendables* (2010), *Hercules* (2014)). In a way, Nu Image and Millenium Films were the next generation of Canon Films. All of his productions are usually not particularly good but have big movie stars like Bruce Willis (*16 Blocks* (2006)), Nicolas Cage (*The Wicker Man* (2006)), Al Pacino, and Robert De Niro (*Righteous Kill* (2008)). Later, many of these films were also made by Emmet-Furla Films, who also benefited from German investor financing. So, I fulfilled the term sheet and flew back to Germany after about a month.

Hannover Leasing had a closed 200 million DM leasing fund with a major studio, so they were no longer interested in my little film. I couldn't believe it and wanted to sue them, but Taunus Film CEO Grass waved this off saying, "We can't sue our own shareholders." Grass suggested that I should pursue the fund idea outside of Taunus Film with my Bolu-Film GmbH, so I met a financial expert from Wiesbaden who got me another term sheet, this time from the Dutch ABN Ambro Bank. I flew to Hollywood again and got another guarantee from Regent Entertainment who wanted to make the film cheaper for around 10 million DM. In the end, ABN would have preferred working with a big studio film, so we were out of luck again.

In the meantime, I looked at private investment advisors who sold ships, airplanes, and other film funds. I set up a fund myself (the Erste Boll Kino Beteiligungs- Gmbh und co. KG.) in order to get investors. I used the prospectus of other funds and copied what they wrote, printing 1,000 investor prospectuses that ran 80 pages apiece. My tax advisor Ralph Etterer was willing to become the trustee and tax advisor. Through another advisor, I got in touch with Hans Wömpener from Bielefeld, who primarily sold ships. He also ran Videal, a film fund out of Hamburg which he was no longer completely satisfied with. He was looking for alternative funds to sell. He told me he wanted 25% commission for every DM he collects. I had no other alternative, even if I thought 25% far too much; 15% would have been more reasonable. I gave him 900 of my prospectuses which made him my exclusive sales agent. Noticeably, his sales team was very timid. Almost all of the money he collected only came from his investors. He was able to get around 10 million DM. When you take away his 25% cut, trustee costs, and tax filings, we had 3.2 million DM left to shoot *Sanctimony*.

Since I would be making the movie in early 2000, I couldn't use the old title End Of The Second Millenium. The sales agents from Regent suggested I revise the script and retitle the film *Sanctimony* instead. He also mentioned I should also fly to Vancouver, BC, because Regent would produce it there with Shavick Entertainment. In Canada, you can get a labor tax rebate subsidy of around 30% from the state. It's also cheaper to shoot in Canada than many other countries. For example, a gaffer in the US would cost $500 a day. A gaffer in Canada would cost $500 Canadian dollars a day, which comes out to around $350 USD. On top of that, we get around $100 back in subsidies. Typically, shooting in Canada costs half as much as it does in the US.

I came to Vancouver for the first time in January 2000 to shoot *Sanctimony*; also over the course of 25 days. Regent brought in some great actors like Casper Van Dien (*Starship Troopers* (1997)), Catherine Oxenberg (*Dynasty*), Eric Roberts (*Runaway Train*) and Michael Paré (*Streets Of Fire* (1984)). My first meeting with the actors for the readthrough was a disaster because at the time, my spoken English so bad that I couldn't have detailed discussions with the actors. Luckily, my cameraman Mathias Neumann had studied in LA and spoke better English than me. He was a big help in improving my communication with the cast and crew. English was always my weakest subject at school. Now, I had no choice; I had to talk to everyone. Shawn Williamson was the executive producer, and we had a good crew.

The shoot went like clockwork. Regent was thrilled with the results. The premiere of the film took place in a cinema in Cannes during the Cannes Film Festival, and Regent made a few good sales. As the first few hundred thousand dollars rolled in, I started paying back the investors. They were pleased to get a return on their investment so quickly!

BLACKWOODS

Wömpenerr wanted to make a second feature with my production company Boll KG, but I counteroffered with him getting a 15% commission instead of 25%. This was not of interest to him. I knew of other financial advisors who could broker my funds, and thought I didn't need Wömpener anymore.

Unfortunately, the new brokers weren't as good as I thought. We only had half the budget, so my second film through BOLL KG had to be done on the cheap. I originally titled it Deadly Trust, but we ended up changing the name to *Blackwoods*. Regent refused to pay the rest of their 60% guarantee due to some flimsy excuses, so I couldn't make this film with them. Instead, I found another distributor with RGH Lions Share Pictures.

Blackwoods had a fun cast including Patrick Muldoon (*Starship Troopers*), Michael Paré, and Clint Howard. My idea for the film was what would you do if you couldn't trust anyone anymore, and even your lover was your enemy? We shot again in Vancouver with Shavick Entertainment. The shoot in North Vancouver's forest took place during the winter of 2001. We often shot in the freezing rain at night.

While we were filming, I met a young actor named Will Sanderson. He became my best friend in Vancouver, and he acted in many of my films going forward. We had a sports competition for years where we played around 20 different sports a year against each other. Tennis, table tennis, squash, running, wrestling, boccia, table football, you name it! I became the champion twice, and he became the champion once. After he played the titular serial killer in my horror film *Seed*, he studied medicine in Texas, got married, and is now a successful doctor in Vancouver.

While *Blackwoods* looks cheap (it was shot in 18 days), it is an exciting thriller that is never boring. We weren't happy with RGH as the distributor from the start, so we pulled it from them and sold it ourselves. In doing so, we were able to make a sensational 59% payout back to the investors very quickly. And it would have been even higher if RGH hadn't stolen some of the money. I later ended up suing them and won. Unfortunately, in the US, the state does not help individuals collect money that has been won in court. It's unbelievable, but there is no such thing as a bailiff for these purposes. If you have a judgment against a company, there is no enforcement against the owners or managing directors.

Over the years, I have been through the legal system in the US and Germany, and both are shit. In the US, you simply do not get your money back. Incorporated or limited legal business entities have zero capital and just file for bankruptcy without any consequences for the owners. In Germany, a GMBH does not protects you either. Managers are immediately held personally liable by the tax office or other plaintiffs. RGH went bankrupt, and then simply opened a different company named Echelon and continued to cheat producers.

Two years later, I met the managing director in the elevator at the American Film Market in Los Angeles and asked him why he didn't pay any of his debt to me. He replied, "Why? It'd be like feeding a dead horse!" In other words, he told me to GO FUCK MYSELF!

The reality is that the only way you can get money from such wankers is to act like the mafia and send people to tear him and his family apart. The prospect of a prison sentence always kept me away from such measures, but I was often on the verge of at least taking some of this sort of action myself.

Right now, nobody is investing in film in Hollywood. All the producers and distributors are constantly looking for others from around the world who want to get rid of money by investing in film productions. Russia, India, and China are now in the spotlight.

Between 1999 and 2005, German funds were the main donors for Hollywood. At least 25 billion dollars came from German tax saving models across the pond with not even 25% of that coming back to the investors.

MULTITASKER UWE BOLL DOES IT ALL

The question I get asked a lot is whether I became an author, director, producer, head of a film fund, chairman of the board of a corporation, managing director of over 10 other companies by choice, or whether it just happened because I never got a job offer as a director and never found a producer who supported and financed me. Why didn't I have a Bernd Eichinger, like Uli Edel, Doris Dörrie or Sönke Wortmann? Why didn't I make any friends in the German subsidy or tv offices? What can I say? It is what it is! My whole life, it has always been me against everyone. Without me taking care of everything, nothing would happen. That's why I didn't give up where others would have thrown in the towel.

I think the endurance and stamina came in during my childhood in dreaming big without a real connection to the film industry I wanted to belong to so badly. For decades, I had read hundreds of film books, written thousands of pages on film, and watched over 15,000 films. I had to change universities twice for my doctoral thesis and my doctoral advisor three times. It took me 10 years to get a real job at a media company, 3 years to finally launch my film fund, then another 2 years to raise the money for it. I had no girlfriend before I turned 21.

Everything was always difficult from the beginning; nothing went smoothly, and nothing came of its own accord. I was not welcomed as a film director with open arms. I was rejected, ignored, and hated by the German film industry (film festivals, funding, and TV channels). Of course, this became more and more obvious the more films I made. Later on, there was envy when I made bigger films with well-known Hollywood actors. The problem later for many people was that they couldn't completely overlook me because I was always very active in the press. Over the years, I also got more and more fans, especially underemployed actors, who always agreed with me because they wanted to work with me. Other directors were jealous of me because I made more bigger budget films than they did.

Now, it's time to review the rest of my movies after *Blackwoods* all the way up to the present.

HEART OF AMERICA

School violence and school shootings are topics that have always bothered me. After the Columbine High School massacre, I wrote a script on the topic in order to show the X factor, the black box that makes people run amok. We shot *Heart of America* with my usual crew in Vancouver over about 20 days of shooting in 35mm. The opening was very complicated because we did a camera shot that was about three and a half minutes long without cutting in order to introduce certain characters into the plot. The Steadicam operator Nathaniel had to start on a crane, from on the first floor and then drove down, then climbed from the crane and went into a house to shoot some dialogue. Next, he got out onto a golf cart traveling to the next house, went back in, and shot the next dialogue sequence. Finally, he went out again across the street, climbed onto a crane, was lifted over a hedge, came back down the other side, and closed in on Elisabeth Rosen, who was sitting on a staircase. It took a whole day to get the entire shot.

In this film, I gave Will Sanderson another role, and his little brother was played by Brendan Fletcher, who later became unforgettable at as the lead Bill Williamson in my Rampage trilogy of films. Michaela Mann, with whom I walk our dogs with to this day, played the rape victim Slow Alice White. Future star of *The West Wing* and *Mad Men* Elisabeth Moss had a small role as a pregnant student. The teachers were played by Michael Paré, Patrick Muldoon and Jürgen Prochnow. The young people acted much better than the more experienced actors.

The best scenes in the film are the rape scene and the scene in the schoolyard where the bullies humiliate the main actor and make him eat shit. The film was very good, my best film up to that point, but it was ignored by all the A-list festivals. Since it was a drama, it flopped financially. I thought this film was first-rate, and so did every I knew who saw it. Unfortunately, that wasn't enough.

Due to its failure, I was very open to Mindfire Entertainment's suggestion to make a film based on Sega's smash-hit arcade game *House Of The Dead* (2003). Firstly, at this point, I had raised around 30 million euros with the 3 Boll Kino Beteiligungs- Gmbh und Co KG thanks to the fact that the other German film funds sucked and didn't return enough money to the investors. My fund was not a smash hit, but it was clearly better than 95% of the other funds. I raised more money and needed larger projects to start making films that could become commercial successes.

HOUSE OF THE DEAD

I knew the video game *House Of The Dead* from the arcades. It was a mindless zombie shooter game, and so was the script. However, I liked George A. Romero's *Dawn Of The Dead* and felt that millions of fans of the game would be interested in the film.

Clint Howard, Will Sanderson and Jürgen Prochnow were cast again. I found the script so idiotic that I intentionally shot outtakes and changed scenes again to be ABSURD or FUNNY. That's why there is a separate rare *House Of The Dead Funny Version* on DVD, but it's only really funny for about 30 minutes.

We shot again in the National Forest in North Vancouver where we build the titular house. Unfortunately, we had a lot of accidents because of the armorer. At one point in the film, Jonathan Cherry, who plays the main character Rudy, was supposed to fire a flare. Unfortunately, the cartridge exploded in the gun, leaving his hand badly burned. This is why he wore his glove for the rest of the film because he had to wear a bandage on his injured hand. Ona Grauer fired a pump-action shotgun into the zoom lens of the camera and the blank cartridge accidentally shot out, piercing the $100,000 lens. Fortunately, the cartridge came to rest just before it hit the cameraman's eye. Another time, I told the armorer to shoot up a flare, and it was supposed to land in front of the house. He shot it over the house, and the rocket landed in the middle of the second unit which burned up some of the plants.

After 15 hours of getting the set ready, we had a rig inspired by *The Matrix* (1999) with 160 still cameras set up for a night shoot. The CGI was done by Elektrofilm from Berlin; they later went bankrupt with good reason. Before we could shoot our first Matrix shot, it was 2:00 a.m. I was close to freaking out because the sun was going to rise around 7:30 a.m. Finally, the guys were all ready to go. The first shot was a stunt man doing a somersault with an axe towards Ona Grauer who shoots him with a shotgun, making him fly backwards. The stuntman was attached to a pull cable. The shot started and worked well until the point where he was pulled back too hard and landed into the cameras. The Elektrofilm guys said they had to measure everything again from scratch, but I gave them a 10-minute deadline instead. Sometimes strong language helps!

For the rest of the sequence, we went through shot after shot every 10 minutes. Some scenes were shot on a new type of round turntable that was about 10 meters in diameter with a 35mm camera mounted on the edge. It rushed around the table at about 80 kilometers per hour. If one of the actors accidentally fell and leaned over the edge, the 50-kilogram camera would tear them apart! It all worked, but an accident happened with the table on another film set where the camera severed someone's arm. Our film was the last to use this table, after which it was banned.

Near the end of the film, the house was blown up with over 150 kilos of explosives. FX expert John Sleep did a good job because the 200-kilo wooden door at the front of the house flew almost 20 meters into our camera.

House Of The Dead was also the only film where I completely changed my shooting days. For three days, the only scene on the shooting schedule was simply described as "the chaos continues".

My AD Bryan Knight was a bit frustrated by this, but I insisted that instead of just spending two days shooting the climactic zombie battle in front of the house, we shoot for a full five days. We used the CGI Matrix set up with the turntable, 3 cameras, 25 stunt people, 100 explosions and over 2000 blank rounds. It was exhausting but also fun. This was my first movie with a real budget of around 7 million dollars where it was successfully marketed and released in 1,400 cinemas. On the first weekend, we hit number six in the USA earning 5.5 million dollars at the box office. The film sold internationally in all countries with good buyers like Metropolitan Filmexport in France, which also co-produced films like *The Lord of the Rings: The Fellowship of the Ring* (2001) and *Resident Evil* (2002). In Germany, Kinowelt bought it, who had also released many big films like *The English Patient* (1996)."

After the success of *House Of The Dead*, it was obvious that we would make more video game films because my investors wanted them. Artisan was bought by Lionsgate, and Steve Beeks from Artisan became one of the bosses of Lionsgate. In Germany, money was being collected diligently through the funds, and Lionsgate wanted to stay in business with me. I contacted video game companies and tried to get the filming rights to world-famous games inexpensively. Before too long, a fan brought me into contact with Atari Interactive, and I was able to make a deal.

ALONE IN THE DARK

The horror-action game *Alone in the Dark* was the basis for our next film, and we had more money at our disposal. We wanted to make this film better and bigger with more well-known actors. ICM's agent David Unger brought us Christian Slater (who got paid $1 million), Stephen Dorff and Tara Reid (who both got about $500,000). All of these actors would now do work for less money, but back then they were still real stars. Dorff was a star because of *Blade* (1998), Slater was a star because of *True Romance* (1993), *Broken Arrow* (1996), and *Robin Hood: Prince of Thieves* (1991), and Tara because of *American Pie*. Before the actors agreed to be in the film, I had to meet them in person for lunch in LA. I do this as a formality. Every time I meet an actor in person, they also agree to be in my movies. I think if they meet you, they will do it unless you don't show up at the meeting like a total idiot.

Alone in the Dark was my first film with a budget of over $20 million, and it was also a big jump into the theatrical leagues for line producer Shawn Williamson and production manager Dan Clarke. By now, we had such a good routine going that it ran well from an organizational point of view. Filming went smoothly and was very well planned. The weak points were the script and Tara Reid.

On the first day of filming, Stephen Dorff didn't want to get out of his trailer because his was 50 cm smaller than Slater's. I grabbed Slater and went with him to Stephen's trailer, knocked on the door, and they agreed to swap trailers. Slater was a team player and he stood in front of Dorff smiling. This made Dorff embarrassed, who said he never wanted a new trailer in the first place. So, in the end, Dorff stayed in his trailer. He also insisted on having his own cappuccino machine; we bought him one, and he never even used it.

Unfortunately, casting Tara was a stupid decision and a big mistake. To this day, I regret not firing her on day one. She's not an asshole, but she gets drunk every night. She can't act well in dramatic scenes, which was shit for our film. I didn't fire her because I thought she had sales value, and if I fired her, she could still keep her $500,000 salary. To add insult to injury, I wouldn't have a replacement standing by. Swapping her for an unknown Canadian actress wasn't a great alternative.

Alone in the Dark's script was written by Elan Mastai, and then rewritten by Michael Rösch and Peter Scheerer. Unfortunately, too many ideas were not fully developed, so I decided to make the action scenes bigger and longer, thereby reducing Tara's dialogue in the film. We also gave Tara a pair of glasses to make her look more intelligent. Of course, that was of little use.

One morning, the driver went to pick up Tara at the hotel, but she wasn't in the hotel all night. Christian Slater didn't come out of his rented house either. When the driver went into Christian's house, everyone was asleep. In the beds were various strippers, actors, and, also, Tara. That same night also led to Ben Affleck and Jennifer Lopez's divorce because Ben was part of the party that apparently started at Brandi's Show Lounge club and ended at Slater's house.

The driver woke up Christian and Tara and brought them both to the set, where Tara was not useful. Slater did his job without any problem. Slater's wife came to visit, and she really wanted to act in the film. Without my knowledge, Shawn put her in a SWAT costume and let her run around in the background of a scene.

One evening, she invited some of the crew, the other actors, Dan, and me to the Italian restaurant Cioppino's to celebrate her husband's birthday. She was only drinking Dom Pérignon and eating caviar. The bill came to approximately $10,000, and she pushed the bill over to my side of the table, saying, "I thank our producer Uwe for the invitation!". If this was L.A., everyone would have paid this bill to avoid a scandal. However, because we were in Vancouver,

I did something altogether different, replying, "Fuck you! I won't pay anything. Goodbye!" The next day, Slater felt ashamed about his wife, but it turned out he didn't pay the bill. In the end, Tara, Stephen, and Dan paid for it. Talk about total bullshit! I told Christian that in Germany, if you get invited to something, it means you will not pay a single dollar for anything. We paid him a million bucks on *Alone in the Dark*, so he could have paid that bill without hesitation.

We were filming over in the Vancouver film studios. The next hall over, director Bryan Singer was filming *X2* (2003), the second X-Men movie. Actually, most of the time he wasn't because he didn't show up on set. The few times he did, Halle Berry was yelling at him. His crew just hung out on our set and still got paid. I heard the rumors that Singer had sex and drug parties with almost adult boys every night and sometimes slept on an air mattress with a teddy in his arms on the set. It's amazing how some directors keep getting jobs even though they are absolute perverts, idiots, and/or drug addicts.

There are two days of filming on *Alone in the Dark* that I'll never forget. The first was when Stephen Dorff had to do another film right after his last shooting day with us and needed to catch the last flight out of Vancouver. We shot for 18 hours straight, but he still missed the flight and flew out at 5 am instead. The second day was the shootout with the monsters in front of the Brittania Mine. In each take, around 8,000 bullets were fired from around 80 machine guns; some of them were 50 calibers, which costs around $1 per bullet. It was so loud that even with earmuffs on, you thought your eardrums were flying out of your head! To date, this day in Vancouver holds the record for the most bullets fired on a film set ever.

Since we raised $20 million for the cinema advertising of *Alone in the Dark*, Lionsgate was excited to release the film in over 2,000 cinemas. After *House of the Dead*, we clearly expected to earn over $20 million at the domestic box office. However, the trailer, poster, and whole ad campaign was not good enough. We only made about

$6 million in the US, which, of course, was a catastrophe for the investors. Christian Slater also did far too little PR for the film. At least *Alone in the Dark* was made from the same fund as House of the Dead, so the investors still received around 60% back on top of their 50% tax refund. In other countries, our film did better. On home video, both films made a killing: *House of the Dead* earned over $30 million, and *Alone in the Dark* earned over $20 million.

BLOODRAYNE

With a new fund came new movies. Boll KG's fourth film was *BloodRayne* based on the video game by Majesco. The usual crew (Dan, Shawn, and Mathias) and I were out in the Romanian countryside for over a week to find the right locations. *BloodRayne* was a much more complex film than *Alone in the Dark* in terms of the actors, locations, costumes, and production design. This time, we were going for the A-listers! Kristanna Loken (*Terminator 3: Rise of the Machines* (2003)) was the perfect Rayne, and in quick succession we booked one star after the other: Michelle Rodriguez (*Resident Evil, The Fast and the Furious* (2001), Oscar winner Ben Kingsley (*Ghandi* (1982), *Schindler's List* (1993)), Michael Madsen (*Reservoir Dogs* (1992)), Udo Kier (*Blade*), Billy Zane (*Titanic* (1997)), Michael Paré, Geraldine Chaplin, and Meat Loaf.

Michael Madsen, who fell out of the plane drunk on the first day, was a big problem right away. He didn't want to come to the set and was in his dressing room alone in the dark. I walked towards him, not finding a light switch. I tried to get his spirits up, saying," I hired you because I thought you were great in the Tarantino films, and that's why I wanted you in *BloodRayne*!" In retrospect, I should have fired him straight away, but I didn't see a way out because we were already shooting in Romania and a replacement would have taken days to find. With Tara Reid in *Alone in the Dark*, what I did was wrong; I should have fired her and cast a local Vancouver actor instead. In this case, I felt keeping Madsen was the right choice. He brought his fucked-up attitude to the screen, but all the other actors hated him because Madsen shot every take as "his way or the highway". Kingsley refused to shoot the climactic sword fight with him. Years ago, Kingsley worked with Madsen in *Species* (1995), and it was a bad experience. Ben Kingsley proclaimed, "If Madsen has a sword in his hand, I'm not on set!" We ended up shooting the scene with Kingsley's stunt double shooting it from behind.

One night at Hunedoara Castle, Madsen came into my trailer with two loaded revolvers that a bodyguard bought off the black market. To make matters worse, he was drunk as usual. I told his bodyguard to grab one of guns, and I would take the other gun out of Madsen's belt. Guiding Madsen out of the trailer, we secured the guns, and Madsen was so drunk he didn't notice. I made it very clear to the bodyguard that he would be fired if I ever saw guns on set again.

Another rare day when we weren't filming, we were all sleeping at a small hotel in the ass-end of the world. I walked past Madsen's room, and he told me to come in. He was depressed and told me his life story. His father was a Dane and a Nazi who always beat him. His sister was an actress, but he wasn't. She filmed him with a Super 8mm camera, bleeding after a fight. He was screaming standing right in front of her. She sent this tape as a demo reel to an agency. The agency sent this tape to Sergio Leone, who was planning his next film after *Once Upon A Time In America*. Leone saw the tape and invited him to New York and wanted to cast him, but then died shortly after. The tape ended up back in LA at the agency of Sergie, which then had Madsen come in and do some auditions. From this, he was actually hired, marking the start of his acting career. While Madsen told me all of this, he drank almost a whole bottle of whiskey, pissed in his sink right in front of me, started to cry, and kept repeating over and over, "Michael Madsen found dead in a hotel room."

Nevertheless, when the film later premiered at the Grauman's Chinese Theater in Hollywood, the only people from the cast who came besides Michael Madsen were Kristanna Loken and Billy Zane. Madsen even brought his sister with him, who had just been nominated for an Oscar for *Sideways* (2004). Not a single actor I have worked with has ever been as intelligent as the roles they played.

Many things stick in my mind from the *BloodRayne* shoot, especially the chaotic and negative experiences. Once, a horse-drawn carriage was flattened by a seven-ton truck, and the horse was torn into a thousand pieces right in front of us. A dog got hit by our car and died immediately right on the spot. Wild dogs were everywhere, and I made sure to feed them regularly. I had adopted my black German Shepherd, Laura, during filming. Daisy, a Kangal mutt puppy, followed Laura and me everywhere. I, too, took her into my hotel, and she lived with me for 14 years. I also saved little Fritz, who was in a river dying. I fished him out, got him to a vet, and returned him to my hotel room. I washed the lice out of his fur and fed him from milk bottle. He was only six weeks old at the time! I found Fritz a new owner and stayed in contact with them. Fritz died 15 years later and led a great life.

The food in Romania was terrible; even the restaurants made me sick! The catering was catastrophic. Every crew member lost at least 5 kilos during the shoot. When I was filming in a monastery, I stood by my cameraman Mathias Neumann. He looked over a street corner at least 100 meters away. He scratched his head, asking, "Do you think my suitcase is standing on the sidewalk over there?" I shook my head, replying "How is that possible? Why would they have it?" We walked over to check it out, and, lo and behold, it was his suitcase. His driver had simply thrown the suitcase out of the car instead of taking it to the hotel. Totally absurd!

When I got back to my small hotel after filming, Laura and Daisy were completely dirty, so I threw them in the bathtub. My room looked and smelled like a barn. I slept and returned to the monastery, filming again until 6 in the morning. The dogs and I were all really dirty. When I opened my room door, I could hardly believe it! Nobody had cleaned my room. There wasn't a single clean towel in the place! Everything was dirty, and no staff was available in the hotel. So, I had to use the dirty and wet towels again, and the dogs slept with me in the bed.

At the craft service, there was only an espresso machine and a few cookies. The catering wasn't edible. Quite often, the food was left out in the rain without a cover, so it poured rain right onto the food.

One time, I found a good butcher, and bought myself a big link of salami. I gave the salami to the catering chef, telling him I wanted him to make me sandwiches out of it every day for breakfast. The next morning, I walked up to him and asked for my sandwich, He shrugged his shoulders. The salami was all gone. They ate it all, and I didn't even get a single sandwich from it!

The last two weeks of the seven-week shoot were back in Bucharest. I ran into Dennis Hopper, who was also shooting a film there. He recommended a small Italian restaurant on the way back to the city, and it was truly great. Too bad that I didn't know about that restaurant eight weeks earlier!

I also must mention the super nice Michelle Rodriguez, who often rewrote the scenes overnight and then showed up on set without explaining her changes to the other actors or to me. I liked it that she was so into it, fighting hard for her character. She also didn't want to die in the film and tried to convince me that her character could survive. In the end, dramatically for the story, she had to die. The shoot of *BloodRayne* created so many horrific and funny stories that we all still talk about it to this day.

Billy Zane informed me about a new company that would be able to get *BloodRayne* into thousands of theaters in the US as long as I could raise the money for the advertising. I could sell the video and TV rights to Vivendi/Universal and only do the theatrical release through Jim Schramm and Romar Entertainment. I wasn't satisfied with Lionsgate's job on *Alone in the Dark*, so I went with Jim and Romar. He visited all the major cinema chains (Regal, AMC, Cinemark) with the trailer and reported that he had booked 2,200 cinemas. We then produced 2,200 prints and delivered them to the cinemas at a cost of about $3 million. Schramm said his advertising concept called for a lot of outdoor advertising (billboards and bus stops ads) plus newspaper ads and guaranteed TV advertising only on cable channels. I checked the Nielsen ratings and saw that the film's awareness level was far too low to succeed. We were only at 42% for awareness and 3% for first choice. To have any opening above 5 million dollars at the US box office, you need at least 90% for awareness and 5% for first choice; awareness means how many people in the United States know that the film exists.

It was already obvious *BloodRayne* would be a flop. It was too late to bring the awareness up without spending another 30 million on TV ads right away, which was money we didn't have. On the opening day, I was shocked to see that not all of the promised 2,200 theaters were showing the film. Furious, I stormed into Schramm's office. The per screen average for the movie was very bad. In order to protect my investors' money, I forced Schramm to immediately cancel all the remaining line items and transfer millions of dollars back to us, which he did because otherwise I would have put him in the hospital. In the end, we produced 1,000 prints too many… What a waste!

BloodRayne ended up doing huge numbers worldwide on home video.

IN THE NAME OF THE KING: A DUNGEON SIEGE TALE

Dungeon Siege was a computer game published by Microsoft and developed by Gas Powered Games, a game developer based out of Vancouver. Around 2003 and 2004, Peter Jackson's Lord of the Rings trilogy was wildly successful, so we originally intended for our Dungeon Siege movie to be a two-parter. Several Hollywood screenwriters were commissioned to make it a major action fantasy film with all the trimmings. In the end, we titled it *In the Name of the King: A Dungeon Siege Tale* (2007).

Kevin Costner was supposed to play the lead role. At that time, he needed another success. I loved his classic films *Dances With Wolves* (1990), *The Untouchables* (1987), and *Robin Hood: Prince Of Thieves*. His manager J.J. Harris was really enthusiastic, but unfortunately Costner was not. Costner called me and wanted to be flown into Vancouver on a private jet, to which I said no. I offered to fly to him over on a regular airline to discuss the film, but he really wanted me to book the private jet for him at a cost of $55,000. What bullshit!

On the phone, he tried to convince me to make his serial killer movie *Mr. Brooks* (2007) instead of *In the Name of the King: A Dungeon Siege Tale*. I explained to him that my investors had already chosen *In the Name of the King: A Dungeon Siege Tale*, and that the movie couldn't be exchanged. That was the end of those discussions! In the end, CAA helped us choose other actors, coming up with Ron Perlman, Matthew Lillard, John Rhys-Davies (*The Lord of the Rings: The Two Towers* (2002)), Ray Liotta, Claire Forlani, Brian White, Leelee Sobieski, Kristanna Loken (*BloodRayne*), Burt Reynolds, and finally, Jason Statham for the lead.

Over the phone, Jason told me on the phone that he hates fantasy films. His manager thought it would be good for Jason to play against type, and Jason listened to him. Costing over $60 million, *In the Name of the King: A Dungeon Siege Tale* was by far the highest-budgeted film I've ever made. Shawn, Dan, Mathias, and I prepped for three months. The actual shoot lasted almost three months on stages in Vancouver and in the forests and mountains surrounding the city. Some shooting days, we had over 1,000 people on the set, which required hundreds of cars, shuttles, and trucks. Logistically, it was the hardest film Shawn and Dan produced to date. We had great costume designers and stuntpeople with Tony Ching (*House of Flying Daggers* (2004)) as our second unit director Tony Ching. It was a lot of fun. Looking back, I consider *In the Name of the King: A Dungeon Siege Tale* and *Postal* as my favorite shoots.

I had the opportunity to repeat scenes 15 times without the normal pressure of time. We had 5 35mm cameras running at all times. Over 180 hours of film were printed, which is a shooting ratio of 1:80; a normal ratio for films is 1:30 at most.

During one action scene (the somersault in the fight against the Krugs), Statham tore his ligaments and couldn't perform for three days. He was a real team player and continued to act with his feet taped up. Statham and the entire cast were just nice, and we had a lot of fun while filming. Only Ray Liotta was a drama queen with his own hairdresser and make-up artist from England. He also didn't like fantasy films, but he wanted to do it for the money.

Burt Reynolds played King Konreid, and also acted like a royal on the set. The Duke, John Wayne, was his role model as a kid, and he was proud that got to appear in a few movies with John Wayne early in his career. He gave me a copy of the soundtrack to *Deliverance* (1972), the best Reynolds film in my opinion. The scene in my film where he dies brought tears to my eyes. I thought it was great, but the critics didn't. He told me that this was the first film in his whole career where he played a character who died. His last shot in *In the Name of the King: A Dungeon Siege Tale* was him fighting in full body armor against the Krugs. We shot him up on a platform swinging his sword. During the shot, he got dizzy and fell off the platform, but a stuntman caught him before he hit the ground.

Another time, we shot on top of a mountain. Dan, Mathias and I flew up there via helicopter first. We were waiting on top of the mountain for the rest of the crew and actors to arrive. The helicopter never came back because the weather had changed for the worse. John Rhys-Davies refused to get on the helicopter because he saw a helicopter crash in another movie he was in. We waited for two hours on top of the mountain with no cell connection. Tired of waiting, we made the dumb decision to climb down the mountain ourselves. Eventually, a helicopter came back up to pick us up. We were still above the clouds and had no clue that a bad storm was under us. The day was over, and we hadn't shot anything, but the next day we finally got everything in the can.

On Sooke Island, which is part of southern Victoria Island, we shot on an Indian reservation. It was the most beautiful location I've ever filmed. The white rocks and blue sea looked amazing, and you can see it all in the film. Every morning, there were orcas on the beach only 10 meters away from the land. There was only a narrow road leading out to the reservation. One evening, an equipment truck tipped and blocked the entire road for hours so that no one could get out. The problem was that the unions insisted that the actors and crew always had a 10-hour break. Those three extra hours ruined this turnaround so that we couldn't start on time the next morning. As a result, I had to shoot faster with the support of the second unit action director Tony Ching, who was merciless. I loved him for it. Whatever I told him, he moved his stuntpeople forward. The crew hated him, but also Jason Statham loved him because he delivered great results. The10 Hong Kong stunt people he brought in were like machines and did whatever he told them. They weren't like Canadian stunt people who collect $1,000 a day and want stunt adjustments for everything they do, like getting shot or falling. If a Canadian stuntman has to fly on an air ramp or trampoline and land dead, he wants a few extra hundred bucks. The question that comes to mind is why don't the stunt people just earn $150 a day like extras and get paid per stunt? As it is now, it doesn't make any sense, but of course it's the way things still are. The best Tony Ching scenes are with Kristanna Loken, where the Tree Woman swings from tree to tree like Tarzan and they capture Matthew Lillard.

The filming was successfully completed, and it went into more than a year of hellish post-production. First, we tried to cut it into two films so that we could get double the money. Sadly, the final cut of the film would have only been 85 minutes per film, which is too short for an epic fantasy. The three Lord of the Rings features were almost three hours apiece. I worked with Fox on the video rights and Universal for the cinema and TV rights. Universal wanted to book theaters through Freestyle because they themselves didn't want to bring the film to the cinema. Both said they only wanted one film, but it should be a maximum of two hours long. That's why today there is both a longer 170-minute Director's Cut and a shorter 124-minute theatrical cut available.

The CGI special effects cost almost $10 million and took for-ever because some companies (especially Das Werk from Germany) delivered catastrophic quality, and we had to redo many of the shots. Other companies like The Orphanage and Frantic did a great job. Jonathan Shore did an amazing job as my post supervisor like always. The music was bombastic by Jessica de Rooij recorded with a symphony orchestra. FOX brought the film into cinemas in Germany and even received a Hessian film award, although I was expressly not wanted on stage. Wolfgang Herold, who did the sound mix in Frankfurt, was onstage instead because he was connected to the state of Hessen.

Although the film opened at number 2 in in Germany, it only brought in $5 million in the US box office on opening weekend. One of the main reasons was that Jason Statham didn't do any PR for the film. He had invitations in Germany to big TV shows like

Wetten Dass and *Stefan Raab*, but he didn't come, which hurt the theatrical gross. I had a good relationship with Statham, met him in LA after the shoot, and later had dinner with him in Vancouver. One night, we went to a bar and tons of girls approached him. He offered each of them 20 dollars to just walk away. That was a funny move, and they walked away for free. So, I thought that we were on good terms, but he still didn't did do press for the film and never answered my emails again. Nevertheless, *In the Name of the King: A Dungeon Siege Tale* was in cinemas in over 20 countries, and was in the top 10 for at least 1 week in each of these countries. Unfortunately, not even 30% of the production costs were made back to investors, and the reviews were unfair.

When I was filming, my girlfriend Christine Öhrling was there. She was supposed to help with a behind-the-scenes documentary. She studied film in Mainz but hadn't been with me for the entire filming process of any of my movies before. Now that she was there for *In the Name of the King: A Dungeon Siege Tale*, I somehow didn't feel so good about us. She also stayed out longer at night while I had to sleep because the filming hours filming were so brutal. After filming, our relationship was kind of empty and ended after a long eight-and-a-half years. At exactly that time, we had planned to move from our apartment into a house in Mainz. I ended up moving into that house alone right before Christmas.

FANS AND CRITICS

Since *House Of The Dead*, there has been a wave of negative criticism against me and my films that have never been equaled. I received everything from personal insults in articles to death threats on Facebook. Many bloggers wrote negative things about me under different names. Welcome to the Internet, where little wankers who still live in their Mom's basement suddenly get feelings of power because they have a say in who succeeds in the public eye and who wasn't. One of these icons was Harry Knowles from Ain't It Cool News, who was often flown in from the major studios and film sets in order for him to give these movies positive reviews on his website.

I saw him twice at the Fantastic Film Festival at the Alamo Drafthouse in Austin, Texas, and also have spoken to him. He was so fat that he drove around in a wheelchair. He told me that Paramount had promised him to produce two films with him where he delivered the scripts and would also produce them. Clearly, he was full of shit and didn't understand that Paramount was just making him feel good so he would write positive reviews for them. They held him back for years and of course didn't develop any movies with him.

What struck me as strange was years later when Knowles was accused of sexual harassment from various women. I don't even know if he would have been able to do that if he couldn't get up from the wheelchair. All these nerds who go to Comic Con and other conventions think the stars or studios are really interested in them. In reality, Comic Con is the cheapest advertising that can be done because all these weirdos use social media like Twitter and Instagram all the time. In essence, they are promoting these movies and shows for free for the studios without even realizing it!

The stars and directors and studio heads are very rich and see these fans as losers who pump their last dollar into all the merchandise. Ever faithful, the fans buy the Collector's Edition Blu-ray box sets, costumes, toys, and other overpriced crap. I always thought that these fans supported me, because I was independent and more like them: an outsider who came from nothing and against all odds and made his dream come true. However, I was mistaken in thinking so because in the end these nerds crawl up Hollywood's ass because they want to be invited to premieres for free looking just as shitty as their idols (George Lucas, Guillermo del Toro, Peter Jackson).

The nerds hate me because I'm the opposite of them. I had the same starting point as they did. My parents weren't rich, and I had no connections to the industry. I'm an example that success in the film business can come from nothing. This pissed off the nerds because, in the end, they are quite jealous. For years, I gave everybody interviews. I attended at least 30 film festivals around the globe and was open to everyone. I didn't have a manager, agent, publicist, or even an assistant. Instead, I invited everyone to talk to me or send me an email, and I always answered everyone's questions; I still do this to this day. Instead of getting respect for doing all this, I got hated and most of them felt superior to me.

The reviews of all my films based on video games were so bad that I decided to change two things moving forward. First, I was going to write my own scripts again and make more films about subjects I have a real interest in. This started with my satirical comedy *Postal*. Second, I asked critics to box me so that I could hit them in their fucking faces without getting sued.

I fought my first boxing match in Spain at the Estepona Film Festival in the middle of the night against a critic from Madrid. The hall was full, and the atmosphere was electric. Since a big boxing event was to take place in Vancouver two weeks later, in which I boxed four opponents in one night, I stayed back in Spain and let him get through the rounds. In Vancouver, we rented the Plaza of Nations. I made a deal with a boxing promoter who also organized other fights that evening. He did the whole setup, rented the venue, and built the boxing ring.

The doctors, and referees were all paid by him, and I was able to keep the money from ticket sales. We had over 1000 spectators, and I beat up all 4 critics who were far worse than I thought. They all got knocked out pretty early. I had trained well, and I was in very good shape again with a lot more offensive power than back when I boxed at Bayer Leverkusen.

At that time when I really boxed in a club, I always thought I was a counter-attacker. In reality, I had an extremely good left jab that was difficult to get past when I used it. Fifteen years later, it worked just as well.

I was also always sparring on the sets of *Seed* and *Postal* with the stuntman Ed Anders, who was a Thai boxer and hit back hard; this prepared me for better opponents. Shortly after that night, I flew to the Fantastic Fest Film Festival in Austin, Texas, where festival director Tim League fought against me in both a debate and boxing match. The topic was on if the independent film industry was dead. I said YES, he said NO. A year before, he had boxed against Michelle Rodriguez who started her whole career with the boxing drama *Girlfight* (2000). I boxed him only with my left hand.

I challenged Michael Bay to a boxing match because I saw a chance to earn money and punch his stupid mouth. Bay is the biggest idiot with his mega-big action films, not because he makes the films, but because he thinks they're really good and character driven. That's pure nonsense because all the good scenes in these films were completely created on the computer, and every line of dialogue was an absolute joke. A year later, I talked to the Shia LaBeouf (*Transformers* (2007)) at a festival in Berlin who confirmed that Bay is just full of himself. After I made several insulting YouTube clips directed at Bay, his lawyer called me and said that he wanted to sue me for millions because I said he was a cokehead. I replied that if he wanted to go to court, I would make him take a drug test. He never called back again.

PHOTOS

Young Uwe with his trusted dog Bodo.

Uwe's maternal grandparents, Sophie and Karl.

Sporty Uwe takes an invigorating swim.

Uwe posing with his handball team.

Uwe and Frank filming on a 16-mm camera.

Uwe, Frank, and Michael enjoying a toast
at the premiere for *German Fried Movie*.

Uwe hits the slopes.

Uwe, cast and crew looking at playback footage from *The First Semester*.

Uwe with Thomas Brügge's lighting crew.

Uwe leaning against his trusty car during his Taunus Film days.

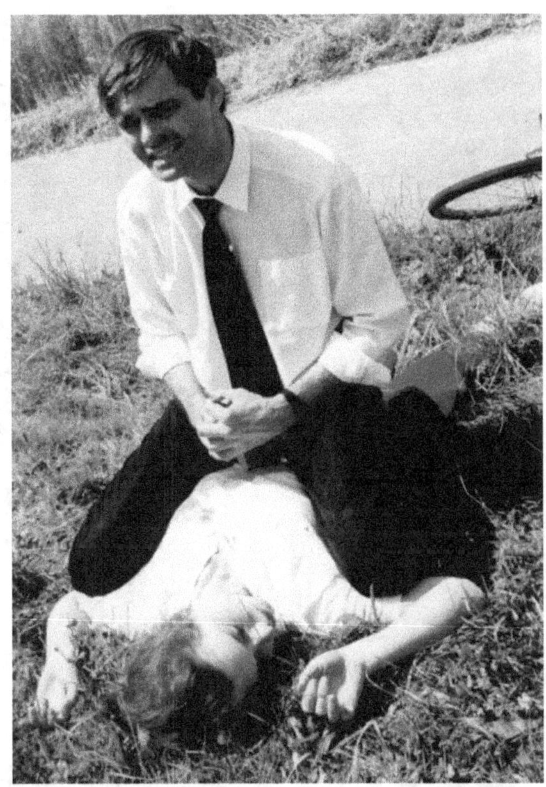

Michael Rasmussen mid-massacre in *Amoklauf*.

Uwe celebrating with his parents.

Uwe and his mother enjoying a brisk walk.

The crew for Uwe's first English-language film, *Sanctimony*.

Kett Turton is about to lose it in *Heart of America*.

Uwe reviews a dramatic scene with Christian Slater in *Alone in the Dark*.

Uwe helps Tara Reid with her pronunciation
on the set of *Alone in the Dark*.

Uwe, Kristanna Loken, and Michael Madsen
at the premiere for *BloodRayne*.

Uwe rehearses a scene with Leelee Sobieski for
In the Name of the King: A Dungeon Siege Tale.

John Rhys-Davies, Burt Reynolds, and Uwe Boll in deep conversation on
the *In the Name of the King: A Dungeon Siege Tale* set.

Uwe posing before his infamous boxing match against the film critics.

Uwe pummeling one of the film critics during his famous bout.

Uwe Boll and Verne Troyer play parodies of themselves
in a satirical theme park scene from *Postal*.

Verne Troyer in Indiana Jones garb for a *Postal* teaser.

The *1968 Tunnel Rats* crew in the sweltering heat.

Uwe on the set of *Far Cry*.

Uwe's intensity cannot be matched.

Sam Levinson in one of Uwe's best dramatic films, *Stoic*.

Attack on Darfur dramatizes real-world
atrocities that barely get reported on in the news.

Uwe goes over a scene with Edward Furlong
and Dan Clarke for *Attack on Darfur*.

Max Schmeling features real-life boxer Henry Maske in the title role.

Uwe with a blood-spattered Clint Howard on a break from
BloodRayne: The Third Reich.

Clint Howard and Uwe smiling on the set of *Assault on Wall Street*.

Uwe hugs a stern Dominic Purcell during
the making of *Assault on Wall Street*.

Uwe, Dominic Purcell, and Erin Karpluk about to shoot one of many dramatic scenes in *Assault on Wall Street*.

Lindsay Hollister is about to lay the smackdown in *Blubberella*.

Ray Liotta and Uwe Boll smiling on the set of *Suddenly*.

A scene from Uwe's searing drama *Auschwitz*.

Uwe chats with Dolph Lundgren in *In the Name of the King 2: Two Worlds.*

A Boll family reunion.

Brendan Fletcher adjusts his aim in *Rampage: President Down*.

Uwe loves dogs on his sets.

Uwe Boll made his triumphant return to filmmaking after a six-year hiatus with *Hanau* (2022), a gripping drama inspired by a real-life massacre.

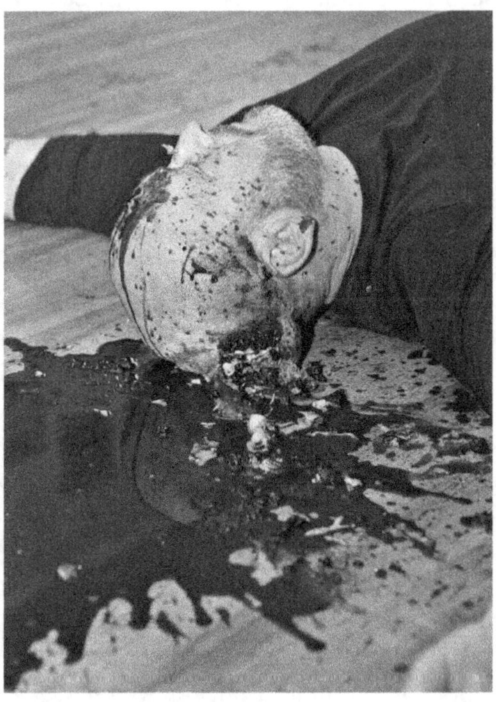

A close-up of Olaf Ittenbach's gore FX in *Hanau*.

Uwe with the stars of his latest film Last Shift,
Anthony Pesi and Kristen Renton.

Uwe Boll, Gino Anthony Pesi, and Willie C. Carpenter
with a dog in *First Shift* (2022).

A collage of posters from Uwe's films.

Patrick Muldoon and Keegan Connor Tracy
in *Blackwoods*, one of Uwe's early thrillers.

SEED and POSTAL

Seed and *Postal* were shot back-to-back. While I was filming *Postal*, I had the boxing matches coming up, so I was always in training while I was filming. Every lunch break, I had a rigorous sparring session with Ed Anders. The killer in *Seed* was played by my buddy Will Sanderson. It was his final acting role. Afterwards, he moved to Texas, got married and became a doctor. This was very good for him because he now earns $300,000 a year.

In the film, Max Seed doesn't talk but he does kill people. Michael Paré plays the cop and former Mr. Universe Ralf Moeller played the prison director. When making *Seed*, I wanted to shock and cross all boundaries. At the same time, I wanted to show my world view: humans are neutral and can be influenced in any direction, so we have no innate morality. Thus, we have no inhibition against killing or torturing. We don't care about the victims, whether humans or animals. Animals kill only to eat or to defend themselves and their territory. People kill for a variety of reasons. Sometimes, they kill for no reason at all.

For the opening credits, I used footage I got from PETA where dogs get burned alive to set the tone for my most brutal and dark film. Many scenes were shot in Riverview, an old insane asylum where a lot of productions are shot despite there still being an active wing full of patients.

One evening, I was jogging on the grounds, and an inmate was standing in the rain peering through a hole in a tree. I could only see him in the dark at the last moment, and I freaked out for a second because he looked so strange. That was very creepy! The *Seed* shoot went without any problems.

Immediately afterwards, I went into pre-production with my film *Postal*. The video game company Running with Scissors from

Tucson, Arizona sold me the rights and a completed screenplay. Their script was just a shooting spree that was not very funny. The game, on the other hand, was very funny. A member of my Uwe Boll Fan Club had written a treatment which I used as a basis for my script. My AD Bryan Knight rewrote my script in better English and got a co-writing credit because he also came up with great new scenes.

In what other film would a cat be used as a silencer? Only in *Postal*! We also made jokes about 9/11, Auschwitz, religion, gays, blacks, handicapped people, whites, monkeys, dwarves, President George W. Bush, Osama Bin Laden, and just about anything else you can think of. Where else can you see Verne Troyer (a dwarf) getting fucked in the ass by monkeys? Only in *Postal*!

Dan Clarke and I flew to LA to hold some casting sessions. Zack Ward came in to audition for the role of the corrupt, racist cop. Dan and I were immediately sure that he was our Postal Dude. As soon as he read it, it came across how he is as a person: he wants success, but he doesn't have it. Zack is desperate with a violent streak, but also has a very good sense of humor. The entire film *Postal* is very well cast, even down to the smallest roles. Great actors like Seymour Cassel, J.K. Simmons, Michael Huddelston, Rick Hoffmann, and Eric Avery really livened up the screen.

We shot on 35mm in 30 days with over 50 speaking roles in 30 different locations. The budget was almost $15 million, so it was a bigger film for me. Even though later critics desperately tried to dismiss it as trash, *Postal* is the harshest and most accurate political anarchy comedy to date in the totality of film history. It's also by far the best video game movie ever made. Only the animated show *South Park* has similar brutally dirty and politically incorrect jokes. Almost all video game adaptations, including mine, are ultimately simple, primitive, and mostly borderline idiotic entertainment, but not *Postal*. *Postal* was written and directed in the spirit of total freedom and the good old saying, "Everything that exists is worth perishing!" No religion, no nations, and no races is the ultimate message that I wanted to convey with *Postal*. It's absurd how much time we still waste in arguments between nations, prejudices about skin color and idiotic conflicts and wars over the question of who has the better God, nation or race. In order to save planet Earth, we have to leave this nonsense behind us and all of us and take care of the important problems like climate change and poverty.

Every day of filming *Postal* had new highlights. We were constantly laughing on set. When the dailies came out of the lab and I played the DVD in the video village, almost the whole crew stood behind me and laughed their asses off. The little Mini-Me Verne Troyer (*Austin Powers: The Spy Who Shagged Me* (1999) and the other actors were in top form, and I played myself as the owner of an Auschwitz amusement park. I often had small appearances in my films in the spirit of Alfred Hitchcock, but it was only in *Postal* was I truly happy with my role. I suppose my second favorite cameo would have been playing Hitler in *Blubberella* (2011).

In our sequence in the Little Germany theme park, we also had a scene in which only children were shot, which was funny for two reasons:

1. It's IMPOSSIBLE in Hollywood movies to kill children, so it's funny that we even equipped the children with blood packs and shot them in slow motion.

2. The Taliban who fired into the crowd only killed the children by accident, which is of course totally absurd, but makes it all funnier.

The Postal Dude's wife was an extremely fat actress (Jodie Stewart) from Texas who was super funny but could barely fit on the plane. Her husband was a normal kind of Texas fat, but she could barely walk. For fun, I shot a scene with her in which I just let her eat super sloppy for several minutes. She ate sausages, cakes, bananas, and cucumbers all mixed together. The scene didn't make it into the movie because it was too disgusting. I really liked the scene where

Postal Dude came into the caravan and caught her having an affair with the neighbor. The funny thing about the scene was, of course, that the neighbor didn't care about getting caught.

Some crew members from my old films didn't want to take part in *Postal* because they either had different political opinions or feared for their careers. What poor idiots! Shawn Williamson also stayed away from filming, but had no objection to his salary, which he received as a line producer. No one wanted to play the window cleaner who was washing the windows in the World Trade Center in the opening sequence when the plane crashed into them. The producer Dan Clarke was game for the scene, and he had a great moment as an actor. Luckily, he had the same black humor as me and had no problems with the content of the film.

I never felt as comfortable in my element as I did with *Postal*. I was again the filmmaker and intellectual Uwe Boll who tells the world the stories that are important like I did with *German Fried Movie* and *Barschel: A Murder in Geneva* at the beginning of my career. *Postal* was indeed the closest thing to my very first film *German Fried Movie*, in which Frank Lustig and I showed no restraint. I still would have loved to have made *Postal 2*, but the financing never came through. You can't make *Postal 2* too cheaply because then the film would be just a little brother and probably a piece of shit brother of *Postal*.

I have already written various scenes for *Postal 2*. The opening would show the murder of Osama Bin Laden and reveal the absurdity that the Americans were too stupid to land a helicopter and then couldn't enter the building because they forgot the key for the door; they end up calling a locksmith who never shows up. The joke here is that they don't even try to blow the door off, which is what everybody would expect.

The second scene would show an ISIS unit beheading hostages, but the ISIS idiots would be ordered around by a film director who was not happy with the whole process. The director would have the whole scene repeated dozens of times until there were no more hostages left. In the real ISIS videos, you can see that they are extremely well filmed, so of course a satirical scene like this is appropriate.

When *Postal* was finally finished (there is also a two-hour director's cut version of the film only available on German DVD), I had a supporter in the head of marketing with Soumya Sriraman from Vivendi/Universal who was a big fan of the film. We decided to release the film into cinemas on the same weekend as *Indiana Jones and the Kingdom of the Crystal Skull* (2008). We made super funny online spots starring Verne Troyer as Indiana Jones and me as General Patton. These spots are still available on YouTube, and I still love them to this day.

Postal also played at a few festivals in Montreal, Austin, and Brussels where it was a big success. Unfortunately, US cinema chains didn't want to show the film, so it only opened in six cinemas very briefly and quickly came out on DVD. In Germany, *Postal* also bombed theatrically, but later turned into a cult classic.

Whenever I'm at a convention or film festival, people mostly want me to sign their *Postal* DVDs. My autograph card, which I still use today, is a still from the *Postal* set in the Oval Office where I'm standing at the desk with Bush and Bin Laden. We also did a premiere with Vince Desi and the video game team over in Tucson, Arizona, where some people in the cinema had real guns with them. Before the film started, I said, "Guys, I see you have guns! If you don't like the film, then please don't freak out!" Luckily, the film played very well, and they were laughing all the way through it. It was the perfect embodiment of white trash.

Postal was also the opening film of the New Jersey Film Festival. The mayor, who was actually supposed to give the opening speech, refused to come because *Postal* was being shown. During the screening, a number of viewers walked out in protest. The tent in which the film was shown was in a meadow directly opposite Manhattan. You could almost see the gap left by the collapse of the Twin Towers.

I confronted some of the protestors outside the tent with my view of 9/11: *Postal* does not make fun of the victims, but of the idiotic beliefs of the attackers, whom I portrayed as brainwashed idiots. Secondly, I also wanted to make it clear that the 3,500 dead were victims, not heroes, and that the Americans' reaction to the attack was completely exaggerated. It was already clear at the time that Saddam Hussein had no connection to Osama Bin Laden. Instead, the Saudis (where Osama also came from) were the financiers of Al Qaeda, only the Americans did not hold them accountable because the oil business was more important to them than getting revenge for the 3,500 victims.

I'm very proud of making *Postal*, but financially the film was a disaster. During filming, I met my first wife, a Canadian of Chinese descent. Pretty quickly, she got pregnant, we got married and had a son. After a few years, the relationship ended. We fundamentally misunderstood each other. My blunt and unpolite personality was not a good match for her. She indulged in a slight depression, hated Germany, and was a yoga teacher (please watch the scene in *Rampage: Capital Punishment* (2014) where Bill Williamson shoots the yoga teacher; that was a warm comment on my marriage!). In the end, we had nothing in common.

In the beginning of a relationship, it doesn't really matter if you are a good fit. If you have the same interests, humor, hobbies, sleep habits and world view, it truly doesn't matter because you are fucking the whole time. After a year or so, all that stuff starts to matter more and more. Between 2013 and 2020, we shared custody of our son 50/50. This is why I stayed mainly in Canada. It allowed me to be close to my son and allow him to grow up with both parents in his life. Since 2020, when I moved with my second wife and second son to Germany, my oldest son comes to visit during his school holidays.

The lessons I learned from this relationship arc crystal clear. You should only seriously move in with someone, get married, and/

or have children if you have 90 to 100% agreement in lifestyle and general views. When do both partners want to sleep? What activities make both partners happy (cycling, hiking, swimming? maybe going out to the discothèque?)? How often do they both want sex? What do they both like to eat? If your partner is a vegan, but you love meat, forget about it and run! If your partner has a night out and likes to go dancing, but you prefer to have a cozy meal and lie in bed at 9 p.m. watching films, then run! That's also the reason why I'm very happy now with my second wife. We checked all the points before we moved in together, and we're 100% compatible. We enjoy eating out and working a lot, but we're family people and prefer to be in bed early and watch TV at home. We do some sports, but not too much, love sex, are very practical, and hate long airplane flights. We prefer traveling to closer destinations and being at home drinking red wine and eating everything that tastes good (organic, if possible).

The experience of this first marriage also led to my conviction that it wasn't worth fighting for a relationship. Of course, this sounds harsh, but is only reflective of my experience. I tried everything again with my first wife a year before the divorce: talk therapy, couples counseling, and all of it was nonsense. Of course, such sessions bring some benefits to yourself, and you try to do everything to make it work again, but at that point the relationship is already over anyway. One of the partners has already left the relationship for a long time, and you can no longer change that. It only costs time and money. If you are no longer in the position to talk to your partner openly and honestly and lovingly without a third person in the middle, you should then leave as quickly as possible like how it's supposed to be handled.

BLOODRAYNE 2: DELIVERANCE

That same year we shot *Postal* and *Seed*, we also shot the second BloodRayne film, *BloodRayne 2: Deliverance* (2007) because we had the money from Vivendi/Universal and German Investors. We successfully received a private placement after the official film funds were completely banned or abolished for tax purposes in 2005. These private placements were only allowed to have 10 to 20 investors, and they had to make all the important decisions in the film's production. After 2005, the big film funds were all stopped by the government. In effect, this private placement system could work as a successful play with the tax office. Somebody else was raising the money (not my company anymore), and I just received funding for 3 or 4 more films before these private placements were stopped. By 2007, it was all over with German private film investors forever.

We decided to set *BloodRayne 2: Deliverance* 100 years after the first film in the Wild West. Kristanna Loken, whose career was now in the toilet, was supposed to play the lead again, but at the last minute her agents were trying to get a lot more money (something like $300,000 instead of $100,000). I made it clear to her that *BloodRayne 2: Deliverance* had a very small budget compared to the first film, and we couldn't possibly pay that amount. She stayed firm, and I had to find a new lead. I ended up casting Natassia Malthe (*Elektra* (2005), *DOA: Dead or Alive* (2006)) as our new BloodRayne. In the end, they're both not great actresses.

The shoots for all 3 BloodRayne films were hard, frustrating, and cold. *BloodRayne 2: Deliverance* was the hardest of them all because we shot at night in freezing rain in a Wild West City Bordertown about an hour outside Vancouver. The gravel road to the filming location had one-meter-deep potholes due to the rain and was almost impassable. Nothing worked on the set. I had cast several actors from *Postal*, like Zack Ward as Billy the Kid, but this time he was just not good.

One night, a gas-heater exploded and shot like a rocket through the roof of a building and landed in another building while it was still burning. Unfortunately, the new building where it landed had 40 more 40-liter containers of gas. We had to run away from the set and leave everything standing there. In the following hours, the fire department came, but they didn't dare get close to the building and we could only watch as one container after another blew up. In total, three buildings burned down, including the train station. I went to Malthe's trailer and opened the door, and she was sitting there listening to music and was totally not aware that outside was a huge inferno. I couldn't believe it!

It wasn't until two days later that we were able to continue filming. We had to reshoot scenes to explain why three buildings were suddenly missing from the city. Finally on the last shooting day, Malthe had to jump into ice- cold water. I made her go in several times so that she almost fainted. It was the last scene that we had to film, so I wouldn't have cared if she had died there.

Years later, I was supposed to film another western there (a remake of *Stagecoach* (1966)), but it fell apart. I was on a location tour for Bordertown again, and the three buildings still hadn't been rebuilt. The owner of the town only collected the insurance money.

In my entire career, I had only made three films in one year twice. This is simply too much. I was totally exhausted and finished both times. I feel shooting two films per year is best if you are both the director and producer. Keep in mind, if you do make two films in a year, the prep and postproduction will overlap. Even a small film needs at least four weeks for prep, three weeks for shooting, and three months for post.

FAR CRY

After *In the Name of the King: A Dungeon Siege Tale* was not really supported in US cinemas, I wanted to take a different approach with *Far Cry* (2008). By casting the German mega star Til Schweiger in the lead, I wanted to ensure a big theatrical release at least in Germany. I locked that in with Splendid Film and Fox. We shot in Vancouver, and I hired a very good action crew. Scott Ateah was the stunt coordinator, and he did films like *I, Robot* (2004), *Deadpool* (2016), and the Oscar hit *The Revenant* (2015) starring Leonardo DiCaprio. For the big car chase, we got 2 VW Touaregs free of charge as product placement. The usual team was together again: Mathias, Shawn, Dan, Jonathan Shore, and Bryan.

Shooting took place over the summer in Vancouver. I also had other German actors appear like Ralf Möller, Udo Kier and Natalia Avelon. Avelon told me before that her English would be perfect, but this was a lie. In the end, she played an Eastern European soldier, so her accent didn't matter. Overall, the video game *Far Cry* made over $100 million in sales. You would think that the film would also be successful, but unfortunately, the film fell far short of expectations. My film fund number 8 with *Postal, Seed* and *Far Cry* remained the worst fund of them all. It was also the last film fund because German laws were changed in 2005.

Filming continued without any problems, and it was one of my films that means the least to me. Til Schweiger had brought his editor with him. While we were filming *Far Cry*, he edited his film *Keinohrhasen* (2007), which I found very funny. I was right when I told him that his film would be a huge hit. He then watched my film *Postal* and laughed his ass off. Unfortunately, *Postal* wasn't that successful. That's life!

Til was a good lead actor, and he was also a filmmaker himself. He showed no attitude on set. He was cooperative and promoted *Far Cry* in Germany on various TV shows, which at least helped the film not be a total flop in my home country.

1968 TUNNEL RATS

For *1968 Tunnel Rats* (2008), we had a video game developed by a Hamburg company headed by Marc Moehring. They had a good reputation as a developer, but then took way too much time to finish their Tunnel Rats video game and eventually went bankrupt. They couldn't even manage to deliver to more platforms than just the PC; it only came out through Steam. Moehring had signed personal promissory notes to both lenders and me that he would deliver the game for the PlayStation 3 and Xbox 360, but he never did. Instead, he filed for private bankruptcy. The game was mediocre at best; its Steam-only release did not even bring back 30,000 euros with a capital investment of around 1 million euros.

The film was shot in South Africa with Chris Roland as executive producer. We shot on location in the jungle near Durban and in a studio at Cape Town. Dan Clarke and I found very good young US actors. One of them was Nate Parker who later became famous from directing, producing, and playing the lead role in *The Birth Of A Nation* (2016), which received $17 million from Fox Searchlight at Sundance with a production cost of $10 million. His film received several awards. My regular actor Michael Paré (*Streets Of Fire*) was there. The rest were unknowns but good actors which didn't detract from the film because it was supposed to come across as more realistic.

The Vietnam War was won by North Korea because they built 180 kilometers of tunnel systems in the jungle. Their guerrilla tactics where they kept coming out of different holes as the Americans attacked them were carried out for years. In *Platoon* (1986), you could sense something general about it, but only my film that put this fight front and center. I wanted to show how bad, absurd, and senseless war is in general, and how all parties of a war will always lose. At the end of wars, there are the ones who died and the ones who survive. Those that live must carry the guilt of the atrocities they carried out.

In *1968 Tunnel Rats*, I tried to show both sides fairly. Both the Americans and Vietnamese are victims and perpetrators, and people die senselessly on both sides just like in any war. This is why none of the main characters survive in the film. I wanted to break the Hollywood cliché that there is always at least one person left alive in the end. The final scene of the film has an American soldier and a Vietnamese woman ready to kill each other. They are buried alive and have to work together to dig themselves out, but both suffocate in the end. This is the CORE MESSAGE of the film: War is always pointless! It is just as Ernst Friedrich titled his book on World War I, *War Against War*. I love Wolf Mahn's song on the same theme, "We Are Deserters - No Country I Give My Life For".

The tunnels were built in the studio in such a way that some tunnels could be flooded, and others were cut in the middle so that the camera could find space right up against the actors. Both the actors and audience alike could feel the claustrophobia and develop the caution required deep in the tunnels where there were mines and hidden traps everywhere.

Before filming started, actors playing the soldiers were trained by a military advisor named Smiley. Stalking in the jungle, weapon handling and hand-to-hand combat were all part of the program. Smiley made it clear that patience was important most of all. In a real war, it only takes one mistake to kill you.

Smiley was a mountain of muscle (2 meters tall and weighing 130 kilos) and had a lot of combat experience as a mercenary. One night, we drove to his house to have a barbecue. Right by the front door were 4 loaded AK-47s that his wife and daughters could have used blindly. There was barbed wire around his property because it was in an unsafe part of town. When the young performers at a disco club got into an argument with locals, Smiley intervened and made it clear to the other group he wouldn't just fight them but kill them if they didn't piss off. They believed him every time and walked away.

Another highlight was that we shot in the jungle, which the locals called Black Mamba Valley. Unfortunately, the black mamba snake is so poisonous that if you can't get to a hospital within 30 minutes of being bitten, you'd be dead. Our nearest hospital was over an hour away; to make matters worse, the paramedics on the scene had no anti-venom because it was not allowed. In the mornings, there were actually mambas in the tents, so we had to send in a squad to get the snakes out. I watched my every step which was harder than it sounds because we were also shooting at night. Once, an actor came crawling out of the tunnel and when I looked at him, I saw a black mamba crawling away. I didn't interrupt the shot because otherwise the panic might have caused the snake to bite him.

We also booked an old army helicopter that had to make emergency landings three times before it finally reached the set. We didn't tell anyone that either, otherwise no one would have gotten on the set. Anyone who knows *1968 Tunnel Rats* knows how great the helicopter opening shot is. It was a great shoot overall. To this day, the film is one of my favorites as it is both important and intense.

STOIC

My movie *Stoic* (2009) is based on a real case in a German prison in Siegburg that both shocked and fascinated me. Three small-time very young criminals raped and tortured another teenager for two days and finally hung him. They murdered him even though they had only committed small crimes before with a sentence of just one or two years. By committing this murder, they ruined their lives for no reason. There was a shortage of staff in the Siegburg prison at the time. As a result, the inmates were not allowed to leave their cells from Friday night until Monday morning. On Saturday mornings, they received all their food at once to last them until Sunday's lunch. It's kind of believable that people could get in a fight in a small jail, but to kill somebody is another thing entirely.

It all started with a card game. At one point, the three criminals all went against the one teenager. They hit him, put his head in the toilet, raped him themselves, and then raped him again with a broomstick. They soon realized the teenager would tell the guards what happened to him on Monday, and they would get in trouble for it. To try and avoid this, they hung him and tried to cover it up as a suicide that happened while they were asleep... What an ingenious plan by total idiots! During the autopsy, the injuries the three criminals inflicted upon the teenager were all found. Everyone confessed and got over 20 years of jail time.

What I found so interesting was the idea of "What are people capable of?" Why are people capable of something like that just because they argue with each other locked in a jail cell?

I wrote a treatment and cast Edward Furlong (*American History X* (1998)), Steffen Mennekes, Shaun Sipos and Sam Levinson (the son of director Barry Levinson who would later creat the hit show *Euphoria* for HBO). They were willing to shoot scenes like a play and improvise their dialogue. We built the cell in a small film studio. I had the actors spend a night in the cell so they could feel what it's like to be locked up.

The next morning, they were ready to go, and we shot the scenes chronologically exactly in the order in which they happened. Two 35mm cameras rolled non-stop with each take lasting 3 to 8 minutes. We could have shot the film in one day, but there were some special effects that took time. These effects included pushing someone's head into the toilet and filming it with an underwater camera and the climactic hanging scene.

The actors all gave very good performances. Edward Furlong was quite sensational! After three days, the filming on the jail cell set was finished. The next day, I played a policeman who interrogates the three perpetrators both in a group and individually to find out the truth of what really happened. In the final film, I am neither seen nor heard. We cut together the guys' answers, and the unmasking worked wonderfully. Everyone tried to blame each other in the end, and everyone claimed to have just been an innocent bystander. When I sent the rough cut of *Stoic* to Sam Levinson, he watched the film with his father and emailed me back, "You knocked it out of the park!"

Of all my films, *Stoic* is the most perfect. It is nothing short of a masterpiece. There is nothing I would change. Nobody else could do it better! In Germany, it was titled *Siegburg*. Only Vivendi in the US and KSM in Germany paid good money for the film. The rest of the world paid pennies for the rights. In the end, *Stoic* lost money.

RAMPAGE

Rampage (2009), the first film in what would become a trilogy, was the result of my frustration at the plot and endings of most films being so completely predictable and boring. I wanted to make a film that didn't let the audience relax and was absolutely ruthless until the very end. It had to be surprising and consistent, a bit like the best episodes *Breaking Bad*… Blunt, brutal and logical.

Brendan Fletcher was perfect for the lead role. Since I liked working with Shaun Sipos so much in *Stoic*, I brought him back as the lead actor's best friend. Matt Frewer and Linda Boyd played Brendan's parents, and Michael Paré played a sheriff. Just like on *Stoic*, we shot with a treatment and left room for improvisation, which worked very well.

Rampage had extremely big action scenes with a lot of mass killings and special effects. When Bill Williamson goes through the city and shoots hundreds of people, we had 20 stunt people on duty in places, all of whom were shot with explosives and squibs. The scene where he remote controls a truck into the front of the police headquarters and then detonates it was shot in two different locations. One was in the middle of a small suburb outside Vancouver. The other was in a parking lot where we actually blew up these replicas of the police station using a van packed with 50 kilos of plastic explosives. Bill is a nice guy but is also a gunman and a ruthless bank robber.

During the location scouting in Maple Ridge (about 15 kilometers outside Vancouver), I went to a bingo hall. It was already well attended on Wednesday mornings. Watching the old people playing bingo, it struck me that they were just killing time waiting to die. In a sense, they were living corpses. I booked the bingo hall with the extras, and this inspired one of the best scenes in the film. It's the only location where Bill didn't shoot anyone because everyone was already practically dead already! I got the best reviews of my career for *Rampage*. Just like *Postal*, it turned into a cult film for genre fans who still list it as one of their top ten films of all time.

ATTACK ON DARFUR

Immediately after *Rampage,* I went back to South Africa where I had an extremely positive experience with Chris Roland shooting *1968 Tunnel Rats.* The crews in South Africa are great as is the weather and food. Even better, it's as cheap to work there as Bulgaria or Romania. The only biggest problem with shooting in South Africa is how long it takes to fly there; it's 21 hours from LA and 12 hours from Frankfurt.

Around eight years after the real-life massacres, *Hotel Rwanda* (2004) was released to great acclaim all around the world. The massacres in Darfur were still happening in the south of Sudan. I wanted to make a contemporary film about to make the world aware of this genocide to help stop all the mass murders from happening. Over 400,000 people, including many women and children, were killed in about 10 years.

The person responsible for these deaths was President Bashir who allowed the militia group Janjaweed to kill all the people. Bashir was wanted by the war crimes tribunal in The Hague. Apart from help from organizations like the Red Cross for the refugees, there was no intervention by NATO, the G8, or anyone. After his presidency, Bill Clinton said everyone regretted not having stopped the massacre in Rwanda. Now, the same shit was happening in Sudan.

The dictators of the Middle East (Gaddafi, Mubarak, Hussein, etc.) who were crushed during the "Arab Spring" were not nearly as evil as Bashir. To put it bluntly, my film *Attack On Darfur* (2009) didn't help anything. Today, over 2.5 million inhabitants of Darfur are on the run. In refugee camps, around 1,000 children and women die per week because they cannot get food or medical care. Bashir is still the president to this day.

We only shot *Attack On Darfur* with a treatment. I got the actors for very little money because they saw the film as important. Even Billy Zane, the arrogant self- promoter who stole Jason Statham's girlfriend, suddenly became a team player. Kristanna Loken and Edward Furlong were all very good. My favorite performance was that of the EVIL Janjaweed leader played by Sammy Sheik (*Lone Survivor* (2013), *American Sniper* (2014)). He has a scene where he flattens a village and kills everyone. The Americans play a group of journalists who want to help the village and visit with some Blue Helmet soldiers, but they are so outnumbered from the Janjaweed that they must run away. A few go back to help, but get all killed with one exception… A small baby survives under a dead body, who is eventually found by Kristanna Loken the day after the massacre.

Both the blood effects in the film and the film itself are very harsh and difficult to watch, but that's the movie is so important. All of the Sudanese roles were played by actual Sudanese refugees we found in the slums in South Africa. One of our casting agents was stabbed while working but survived.

One night, two young black men tried to break into my rented house. As they climbed over the wall, I stood on the balcony and talked loudly on my cell phone, acting like I had the police on the line. I actually had no clue what the number for the police in Cape Town was. The intruders believed me, retreated back down the wall, and left.

These Sudanese women who were raped in real life played characters who were raped in the film. They had to act out the painful experiences on film they experienced in their real life. These scenes were very moving scenes and moved everyone on set.

At the end, when we burned down the village, there was a lot of heat. Tons of snakes, scorpions, mice, and spiders crawled out of the earth and ran past me. I hadn't seen anything like that before!

I tried to contact George Clooney, Matt Damon and Brad Pitt to support my film, but only Terry George and Ron Howard watched the film and gave me positive feedback. It was strange and showed all the arrogance of the superstars. This is especially true of George Clooney who is active in the news trying to help the cause of Darfur. We sent each of them DVDs via Federal Express to their agents, managers and lawyers as listed on IMDB Pro. I even placed a full-page ad in the form of a personal letter in The Hollywood Reporter which cost me $8,000.

Despite all these efforts, the film's release remained a quiet one. The film was sent out on DVD, TV stations, and streamers. *Attack On Darfur* was a financial flop. In the end, it didn't help anyone in Sudan except for the refugees who we paid for acting in our film. We also collected money for two women from Sudan who acted in the film so they could get out of the slums and go to a school to become nurses. *Attack On Darfur* is a great film that triggers the most emotions out of all my films. winning an award for Best International Film at the New York International Independent Film and Video Festival.

THE FINAL STORM

A Fox employee came up with the idea for *The Final Storm* (2010), a sci-fi thriller. Shawn Williamson, my line producing partner over at Brightlight Pictures in Vancouver, was able to secure over $2 million in film funding from Telefilm Canada. This made Shawn an actual co-producer of one of my films for the first and only time. Luke Perry (*Beverly Hills, 90210*) and Lauren Holly (*Dumb and Dumber* (1994); she was one of Jim Carrey's ex-wives) starred with Steve Bacic. We shot about an hour outside of Vancouver on a lonely farm. We also closed entire streets for filming in Squamish, which is about 25 minutes from Whistler Mountain where some events in the 2010 Winter Olympics were held.

The budget was almost $5 million total, so the production value of the film was high. Basically, the story was that it was raining all the time. Parts of the world were flooded, but then, suddenly, all the humans vanished except for a farmer and his family. One night, a stranger visits the farm (played by the late Luke Perry) who turns out to be a mentally ill killer. There's a final battle between the killer and the family. At the very end, the earth is sucked into a black hole.

The Final Storm played more like a TV movie of the week, which is how it was sold. In the US, it did extremely well on VOD. Unfortunately, DVD sales and worldwide sells were not nearly as strong. I had a lot of fun times with my three dogs on set: Daisy from Romania, Laura, and Boomer, my first son's dog. Boomer, in particular, farted nonstop and filled the whole house with a stench. I even made a $50 bet with Chance Minter (one of the film critics who I boxed and then hired as an intern) that he couldn't stay 10 minutes in a car with Boomer with all of the windows closed. I won the bet.

I love doing bets like this!. In South Africa, I did a bet with the AD Trevor that he had to drink a bottle of red wine within 60 seconds and then not throw up for 5 minutes! He won that one. On the set of *BloodRayne: The Third Reich* (2011), it was 2 in the morning. I bet a make-up artist $100 that she couldn't drink an entire bottle of vinegar. She gulped it down and had to go to a hospital the next day. Sooooooo stupid!

MAX SCHMELING

Max Schmeling (2010) was completely financed as a private placement by two doctors from Northern Germany with Hessen and DFFF funding on top. The doctors reaped their tax advantages from their investment! The producers really were involved and approved the main actor, former boxing world champion and Olympic Gold Medalist Henry Maske. There were two factors in the project that appealed to me in addition to the money. The first was that I love boxing and boxing movies (*Rocky* (1976), *Raging Bull* (1980)). The second was this would be my first opportunity to film again in Germany in my native language in over 20 years. I immediately thought of Henry Maske as the main actor because Max Schmeling said himself in an interview that his friend Henry should play him if a film was ever made about his life.

Maske now owned six or seven McDonald's in Leverkusen and the surrounding area, so he lived close to my hometown of Burscheid. I met him in his office, where there were lots of trophies and world championship belts hanging about. He said he was interested, and I insisted that he be trained in Cologne by an acting coach. I had Henry work with famed actor and acting coach teacher Arved Birnbaum for a few weeks. Afterwards, Arved reported back to me that Henry was doing very well. Maske brushed up on his boxing to get fit for the film. He also took his acting very seriously. The reason why he was a world and Olympic champion was because of his hard work ethic.

Despite an all-star German cast (Heino Ferch as the trainer Max Machon, Susanne Wüst as Anny Ondra), film funding agencies such as Berlin, North Rhine-Westphalia, Bavaria and Hamburg rejected us. This was only because I submitted the film myself. If Nico Hoffman had submitted the project, he would have been hit with money from all the subsidy stations in Germany. Berlin and Hamburg, in particular, would have had to support such a project because Max Schmeling was a native of both cities.

We had to shoot the film in Croatia for cost savings and found a partner in Jadran Film in Zagreb who had everything: World War II uniforms, old vehicles, the works! Paffen Sport in Cologne had old training equipment and vintage boxing gloves. Adidas made us custom retro shoes and boxing gloves as well.

The film was shot with great media participation. ARD was also involved in the filming because they showed the Sauerland Group's boxing events and Henry was their boxing expert. Nevertheless, ARD didn't want to buy the film. Neither did RTL, who had great viewership from Henry Maske's final boxing matches. In the end, we were able to get the film sold to ARD through the MDR network out of Eastern Germany because Henry grew up in the DDR. We got 700,000 euros for broadcast rights, yet the film was neglected and only aired in the middle of the night after a boxing broadcast on Saturday at 1:00 a.m. This was an absolute joke and an utter waste of the money they had paid us. The film should have been shown at 8:15 p.m. on Saturday before a boxing match, then it would have had 5 million viewers easily.

The filming took place with my typical crew: Bryan Knight as AD and Dan Clarke as Line Producer, although neither of them understood German. Mathias, as always, was behind the camera, and Jessica made the music. We started with the boxing scenes, where were shot in the Arena Zagreb, putting hundreds of extras around the ring. Maske stood for eight hours every day in the boxing ring for five days a week. We shot the matches with a super slomo camera at 1,500 frames per second along with other techniques. The rest of the film was shot on 35mm.

I had a lot of fun even though our crew, the Croatian crew, and our actors liked to discuss everything in detail. The whole shoot went smoothly. The fight, war, and training scenes were shot on the Croatian coast and in Zagreb for the Kristallnacht scenes.

Afterwards, we moved to Wiesbaden, where we shot rural and domestic scenes with Max and Anny. Susanne Wüst was a little drama queen who got worse and worse during filming. Unfortunately, Henry caught the drama queen bug. By the very end of the shoot in Wiesbaden, I was sick of this behavior. There was a group of fans that wanted his autograph. They stayed around for hours, but he refused to sign anything for them. I told him that he was being an asshole for not signing their photos, so he finally gave in.

The highlight was when the Hessian Prime Minister Koch came along and threw a party in the State Chancellery for us in the evening (all at the expense of the taxpayers, of course!). Henry didn't come at first even though all of the guests were waiting for him. I couldn't understand it, so I called his room and demanded he get his ass to the party straight away. He eventually showed up quite angry and greeted everyone at the party.

We edited the film in Munich with Charles Ladmiral, who had also edited Til Schweiger's hit comedy *Keinohrhasen*. The mixing was done by Wolfgang Herold. We applied for funding for a theatrical release but were rejected. My German buyer KSK paid Senator Film to release the film in some movie theaters, but the film flopped. I actually understood why it didn't do well. The film is overall something for an older audience who only watches TV. They wouldn't go to see it in cinemas because it was only shown past midnight.

One funny story from the set was when I had a visit from a rich Russian woman in Zagreb. She emailed me saying she was a big fan of mine and would like to get to know me. She insisted that her father was wealthy and could finance dozens of films for me. At a dinner we all had with the actors, she proposed having a threesome with Susanne Wüst and me.

Anyone who knows me knows that this situation was disgusting to me. First off, I was still married to my first wife at the time. Luckily, she was only in Zagreb for two days, so that part wasn't as awkward as it could have been. In short order, she wrote me an email insisting I fly to Saint Petersburg to meet her father, who would then sign over his first $5 million film contract to me right then and there. My greed for more film financing overtook me, so I flew to St. Petersburg and stayed in a hotel that she recommended to me. The hotel was had 300 rooms, but only one other person was staying at the hotel besides me. I felt like I was in *The Shining* (1980). I wanted to return home as fast as I could. Quickly, I barricaded my door and searched the room for bugs and cameras. I had to take the ferry downtown, but first I checked out the Hermitage because that's where the Tsar lived. St. Petersburg is also known as where Putin came from.

I met her in a bar, and she brought me the signed $5 million contract and said her father was coming to meet us later, but he never showed. Instead, there was a twist that could hardly be true. She got a call because her daughter had suddenly disappeared. Her daughter? Marina Sosnenko only was 24… How come her daughter never came up before?

Her story got wilder and wilder. She claimed her father struck with a vase by her ex-husband, the daughter's father, and was admitted to the hospital. That's why he couldn't meet me, and she had to go back home immediately. That was the last straw. I saw the sights in St. Petersburg by myself and flew home the next day with a signed contract. When I tried to get the $5 million, she now said the money was frozen and her father was near death. She promised after he died, she would inherit $50 million. Later, she claimed in an email she was getting married to Tim Curry (*The Rocky Horror Picture Show* (1975)). In her next email, she said she was in a psych ward. I had to block her emails and call it a day. If you want to make films, you need to go down every avenue to raise money.

In Turin, there was another unbelievable film financing story I had with my colleague Matthias Triebel. Italian businessmen wanted to invest in a film but only with cash. They also wanted to collect a fee for their investment. We met them in a mafia-style pizzeria, but they were just talking out of their ass. As soon as we got home, my friend and lawyer Prof. Dr. Hanno Kämpf took over and had a few phone calls with them, but it became increasingly clear that they wanted to sell us counterfeit bills. A few months later, the gang was arrested. Some people fell for their ruse paying 50,000 euros in fees and only to receive 5,000,000 euros of counterfeit money in return.

BLOODRAYNE: THE THIRD REICH, BLUBBERELLA and AUSCHWITZ

BloodRayne: The Third Reich, Blubberella, and *Auschwitz* (2011) were all shot in one go in Zagreb, Croatia. During our shoot for *Max Schmeling*, the head of Jadran Film Vinko Grubisic was relatively easy to work with. However, our relationship was now becoming more problematic for the both of us thanks to the smaller budgets and tighter schedules we had to work with. The plan was to shoot *BloodRayne: The Third Reich* back-to back with *Blubberella*, then do *Auschwitz* at the end.

This shoot was like all my other BloodRayne shoots, hard and shitty. We had very cold weather, night shoots, bad food, and a kind of hostile relationship with Jadran Film. One night, our office safe with approximately 30,000 euros in it was stolen. Our money messenger who came over from the bank was almost robbed. The police saved him at the last moment.

The story for this BloodRayne film was pretty stupid for me. I didn't really enjoy making it either, which is why I wanted to shoot *Blubberella* in parallel. *Blubberella* was a parody starring a fat BloodRayne played by Lindsay Hollister. I had worked with Lindsay before in *Postal*, where she was very funny in the job interviewing scene asking Postal Dude, "What is the difference between a duck?"

The problem, however, was that the shoot was already very hard, and we only had about an hour each day to shoot scenes with Lindsay. As a result, she had to be in costume waiting around all day. Accordingly, her mood sank lower and lower because she realized this movie wasn't going to be particularly good.

Other actors in the film like Michael Paré, Clint Howard, Steffen Mennekes, and Natassia Malthe had fun shooting their absurd scenes, but they were occupied during the day shooting the regular

BloodRayne: The Third Reich film. The only full day we had with Lindsay was when we shot her apartment scenes. Part of these featured my cameo as Adolf Hitler. The story takes place in World War II where she plays a resistance fighter. Hitler gets mad at her, but then visits her apartment, and they become best friends.

In the end, *Blubberella* flopped badly. Out of the 90-minute running time, only 30 minutes were truly funny. The rest was shit.

I felt *BloodRayne: The Third Reich* was better than *BloodRayne 2: Deliverance*. It more sex (Malthe had a nude lesbian scene), more violence, and better action. I was annoyed that Natassia Malthe and Brendan Fletcher were dating. They acted like they were Brad Pitt and Angelina Jolie on vacation and made a fool of themselves with their behavior. The whole crew, especially Dan Clarke and me, were sick of it. I also missed my son and dogs who were away at home.

Yet again, a Russian woman showed up who claimed to be a millionaire's daughter. She wanted to play a part for free. I gave her a tiny part because I thought maybe her father might invest in my future movies. She had no intention of having sex with me, but just wanted to have a career. I didn't think her acting was particularly convincing. After the film, I stayed in touch with her to see if her father would invest in our films. I saw her again at the Moscow Film Festival where *Max Schmeling* was showing. She had her own driver and was accompanies by some Russian politicians with her. We drove straight on to the cinema with the blue light on like the police do blasting through traffic without getting any tickets. No money came in, and I never met her father.

I gave her another small role in *In the Name of The King 2: Two Worlds* (2011) to keep in touch. Later on, she moved to LA and invested in her own projects. They all flopped. I wanted her money and could have given her a supporting role, but she wanted to play the lead role, which would have been terrible. That's how it is as a film producer. You must stay focused on the MONEY, but most of the paths you take end up being dead ends.

One day in Zagreb, we shot on a snowy mountain where everything went wrong. We filmed the attack of the Nazi convoy on a one-way street that went about 10 km up the mountain to a ski resort and down the other side. We rented the street so that we could drive up and down on just one side. When we started turning around, we could see more and more cars coming up the street with skiers who wanted to go to the ski lifts even though the police had closed the street down there. This made it impossible for us to turn around our big military trucks! There was only light until 5 p.m., and we still had to do a big stunt with a car that went off the track, rolled over and exploded.

I hired my special effects guy from *1968 Tunnel Rats* and *Attack on Darfur* from South Africa, and he did a great job. Of course, this was much cheaper than bringing in a local Canadian effects specialist. In the end, it all worked out.

Now, I was able to get to *Auschwitz*, the film that I really wanted to make. Nobody wanted to make it with me. Dan Clarke didn't find it particularly motivating to make a film that basically shows a day in Auschwitz from the train to the oven to people in ashes. I always thought that only the documentary *Night and Fog* (1956) really showed what an incredible killing machine the Holocaust really was.

Films like *Schindler's List* (1993), *Life is Beautiful* (1997), and *The Boy in the Striped Pajamas* (2008) always told some kind of heroic story. My film shows the killing at the core of the Holocaust. Forty percent of the people who arrived in Auschwitz were killed on the same day. Auschwitz was a slaughterhouse for people: they were sorted out, gassed, and burned without any empathy or emotions. It was total madness, which is exactly what I wanted to show. My film was meant to be a document for future generations as it was becoming more and more apparent that people had no idea what the Holocaust really was. About 80% of humanity has no idea what happened in Auschwitz. This is why I really wanted to show the KILLING itself with several gas chamber scenes. For this purpose, we had to find extras who were willing to act completely naked in the gas chamber. This wasn't so easy, so I put on an SS uniform and made sure that the extras took off their clothes. Before I took played an SS Officer, extras kept going into the gas chamber in their underpants which didn't work out. I had to act in the film to make sure they were getting undressed.

I had also booked a German actor with his little son, but neither of them could act, so I had to omit most of their dialogue. We modeled the boy's body with a photo-realistic dummy we could use to burn in the oven for a scene. It was very convincing!

The shoot for *Auschwitz* only took three days and was very intense. In the end, all the crew members understood better why I was making it. As soon as I was back home in Germany, I wanted to film interviews with students in schools to see if they still knew about Auschwitz. Almost no school wanted me to shoot these interviews for the fear of their students coming across as being clueless about the Holocaust. When I went to high school in the late seventies and eighties, our country's history was instilled in us. Apparently, German schools are already removing World War II history from the school curriculum. If this is the case in Germany, what about India, Africa, or South America?

My brother is a teacher and helped me find kids from two different schools. One was in an upper-class neighborhood and the other was in a lower-class neighborhood. The end results were quite interesting. Students in the lower-end school knew almost nothing about the Holocaust; some had seen *Schindler's List* and now thought Auschwitz was a company that manufactured cooking pots. In the upper-end high school, about 50 % of the students had good knowledge on the Holocaust, and the other 50% knew very little about it. The film was denied by all festivals, which led to a screening at the Berlin Film Festival to compete against the Berlinale who refused to show *Auschwitz*. We showed the film at the Babylon in Berlin where a lot of people came.

I also filed a criminal complaint against the Berlinale Chef Dieter Kosslick. Thousands of films are submitted to the Berlinale and other festivals every year. In order to submit their film, filmmakers must pay a submission fee of 150 euros. All of this money is then used just to throw nice parties for the movie stars. Most of the films never get selected for anything. All the festivals pick which films will be screened and invite the filmmakers to the screenings. Any festival I ever submitted my films to refused to play them. The dozens of festivals I did show my films at, I didn't submit my films to. Instead, the festival managers invited me personally to come show my movie. I consider this fraud because you have absolutely no chance of being accepted unless you are well known, or the film festival managers know you. It's always the same pool of directors getting invited! To make matters worse for independent films, the film subsidy offices and major studios occupy the top spots at the A-list festivals.

Nevertheless, *Auschwitz* did well on DVD and VOD, especially in the US. *BloodRayne: The Third Reich* also played well worldwide on DVD. I even wanted to make a fourth BloodRayne movie set in the modern day, but the video game company Majesco felt my $100,000 fee for the movie rights was now too low. Instead, they asked for $500,000, which was far too much. That was the end of my series of BloodRayne films. Later, Majesco went bankrupt, and another company took over the rights. They too refused to sell me the movie rights to BloodRayne.

IN THE NAME OF THE KING 2: TWO WORLDS

Since *In the Name of The King: A Dungeon Siege Tale* did very well on DVD and on TV around the world, it made sense to shoot a direct-to-DVD sequel with a budget of around $5 million for 20th Century Fox. We mainly shot *In the Name of the King 2: Two Worlds* in the Golden Ears Park about an hour away from Vancouver. We also made it a time travel film with a few scenes set in the modern day.

Dolph Lundgren was of course no replacement for Jason Statham, but with a fee of $250,000, he was cheap enough and had star appeal as an action hero. After he arrived in Vancouver, we discovered he wasn't a good actor and could barely walk. He claimed a knee injury, but in reality, he had both hips replaced recently. Even for a light jog, we had to use a stunt double, which was annoying. We also had Natassia Malthe on board due to her credits in my BloodRayne sequels, *Elektra*, and *DOA: Dead or Alive*.

Dolph hardly drinks. When he does, he prefers Fernet-Branca, a disgusting bitter. He is very intelligent but doesn't talk too much; this is true both in his films and in his personal life. Years later, I also got a hip replacement. I now know how painful the first weeks after the operation are. I'm sorry he wasn't honest about his operation, and that I was so frustrated at the time about his handicap.

What remains fresh in my memory about this film are the accidents. It started out as something fairly harmless when a little stuntman got knocked out in an explosion and had to go to the hospital. He was unconscious for five minutes, but overall did OK. On the second-to-last day, we had a terrible accident with gas heaters exploding. We were sitting on the set by a lake and wanted to go turn around when we saw an explosion right at the catering tent in the trailer. We heard a loud boom followed by a huge fireball rising up right above my car. We ran to the spot and heard some screaming. We actually saw some extras on fire running around. We extinguished their burning clothes and hair with our bodies, rolled everyone on the ground, and started administering first aid. Nobody was critically injured, but there were some nasty burns and shocks. The news helicopters came faster than the police and the ambulances. Our whole shoot came to a standstill.

What actually caused the accident was as follows... The gas containers were refilled by a company on the set. It's too bad they did it in the middle of the catering tent where several heaters were still burning. One of the hoses caught fire, leading to the explosion. It was similar to what happened back on the set for *BloodRayne 2: Deliverance.*

Dan Clarke didn't want to continue filming, but I warned him about December 22 coming up. By December 23, all the actors would fly out for Christmas break and not be able to return for filming without getting more pay. We still had four hours left to shoot and then the film was in the can. Since all the injured people had been transported away to the hospital, we went ahead and finished the shoot right on time.

My car was charred all over, and the radio display on the inside no longer worked. There must have been something seriously wrong with the electrical system. Nevertheless, I was still able to drive home. The injured people were all insured through the film and got compensation. I got a measly $2,000 for my car, which was a total joke because it was a VW Touareg.

In the Name of the King 2: Two Worlds turned out OK. It did well enough with Fox distributing it in around 20 countries. It did splendid in Germany, so it was worth making a third film in the series. Before making a third one, I wanted to make a more personal film about the banking crisis.

ASSAULT ON WALL STREET

The 2008 banking crisis and the subsequent bailouts were a topic that I was particularly interested in because it shows how the rich get richer and the poor get poorer. Corruption is a big topic. Millions of people lost their homes in the financial crisis, and yet the bankers were not punished for gambling with people's finances and investments. Trillions of dollars were lost and hardly anyone went to prison for it. If you rob a gas station and steal $200 in the US, then you get 5 to 10 years in prison. If you lose $300 billion, you still get a settlement, like Richard Fuld from the Lehman Bros. did with a $400 million golden parachute after losing $80 billion.

I wrote down a scenario that reminded me of *Falling Down* (1993) but specifically related to the financial crisis. Like so many of my films, *Assault on Wall Street* is a revenge story that, dealt with political themes and mass shootings. Why does someone in the US run amok for no reason every week, but no banker ever gets shot? Three million Americans had lost their homes and had good reasons to run amok on Wall Street. Thousands of people killed themselves. In *Assault on Wall Street*, my main character loses all his money, his job, and his house. To make matters worse, his wife also kills herself. He decides to kill the people responsible. It is my belief that if proper laws are not applied in society, then there is no need to adhere to them. Too many lower- and middle-class people are being ripped off by those who are above the law.

The film was shot mostly in Vancouver with three days shot on location in New York City around Wall Street. It looks very high quality. *Assault on Wall Street* is a true theatrical film, far better than Oliver Stone's sequel *Wall Street: Money Never Sleeps* (2010). Since my movie only had B-list movie stars, it only came out on DVD. In our cast, we had Dominic Purcell (*Prison Break*) giving the performance of a lifetime. Erin Karpluk played his wife. The villain of the piece, the banker boss, was played by John Heard (*Home Alone*). Keith David, Michael Eklund, Michael Paré, and Edward Furlong rounded out the cast. John Heard was quite sensational in his role as an ice-cold Wall Street villain. Even though we only had 2 days with him, he did a 10-page scene with no problem in a single take.

Dominic Purcell became my friend during the shoot. He has the same political leanings as me and is also a big boxing fan. In some cinema screenings in New York and Germany, the film had a great reception and generated fantastic discussions among the audience. Slowly but surely, it became clear to me that no matter what films I was making, there was no longer going to be a big breakthrough for me as a filmmaker. Bloggers and journalists still thought I was the worst filmmaker of all time. Even though I had made at least five great films since *Postal,* their opinion of me hadn't changed since the *BloodRayne* days. To make matters worse, the DVD market was now going down the toilet worldwide. The VOD market now had streamers like Netflix who were hardly paying anything for fully produced films. Since I also sold the films myself with my friend Michael Rösch as a team, we knew that the market for independent films was over. If a great film with action and a good cast only brought in 50% or less of the budget, then it was all over for smaller films. Only TV, subsidized films, and very expensive comic book movies could stand a chance anymore.

SUDDENLY

Suddenly (2013) is a remake of a 1954 thriller of the same name that starred Frank Sinatra and Sterling Hayden. I was given the opportunity to direct the film by paying a sales guarantee of $300,000, thereby taking over world distribution rights. Producers Robert Bassler and Kirk Shaw were behind the project. Overall, we ended up losing a lot of money because we didn't recoup the budget. I was able to get my 300K back, but nothing more… At least I didn't lose money!

It's too bad, because we had a great cast. Ray Liotta played the cop (played by Sterling Hayden in the original film) and Dominic Purcell (Frank Sinatra) played the top gangster who wants to assassinate the president as he travels through a small town. His fellow gangsters were played by my buddies Tyron Leitso and Michael Paré. Ray's girlfriend was played by Erin Karpluk, who had just played the female lead role in *Assault on Wall Street*. Ray's sheriff colleague was played by another one of my regulars, *Rampage* star Brendan Fletcher.

We shot in Squamish, a little town during the winter in front of the ski-resort Whistler Mountain. I drove an hour each way from Vancouver to the set so I could sleep at home in my nice bed. For the first time in years, I didn't have my regular DP Mathias Neumann. Instead, I had Brendan Uegama. He was young, slow, and deliberate. Every day, he got on my nerves with his nonstop questions.

It was a cold and snowy shoot; only the *Blackwoods* shoot was colder. This time, Ray Liotta was easy to work with and was more in his element playing a cop. He had no problems on set and got on well with Michael Paré.

The original film ended with the president going through the city on the train, and the gangster shoots the cop. We wanted to make our version more exciting. This time, the president arrives via a car convoy and Purcell almost manages to shoot him, but he's stopped and killed by Liotta in the last moment. *Suddenly* turned out to be not so bad. It felt like a TV movie of the week with a great cast. In some markets, they renamed the film as *Operation Olympus* to capitalize on the films to capitalize on bigger budget thrillers like *Olympus Has Fallen* (2013) and *White House Down* (2013).

The Nasser brothers had produced all the Steven Seagal films back in their heyday when they were still theatrical releases. One of them, Jack Nasser, even went to prison and Seagal threatened him when he left the company. Joe Nasser is an unsuccessful actor who prefers to walk around Hollywood with his gun at his side. Now, they just make low-budget shit films and are sinking into no man's land.

They wanted to shoot another film with me and had Christian Slater and Tom Berenger attached. I told them several times that my relationship with them was over. On top of all this, they were going bankrupt. Because *Suddenly* was too expensive for them with a budget of 1.2 million, they brought Kirk Shaw on board. Kirk had produced tons of films for years in Vancouver until the Canada Revenue Agency did an audit and asked him to pay millions of dollars back. The millions in labor tax rebates he got before were disapproved years after the films were shot. Was he right or wrong? I don't know. The fact is, he still makes films to this day.

Both Kirk and the Nasser brothers said that I was the best director they had ever worked with. We never worked together again, and I'm okay with that. Most of their films got cheaper and cheaper. Some of their directors only got 5k as their salary for making a feature film!

At this point, I also got Dani Elias, an agent with Integral Artists who was based out of Vancouver. He hasn't given me a single job to date, even though there are around 50 TV series and 50 TV movies filmed in Vancouver a every year. Nobody ever wanted me in this industry as a director. Years before Paradigm was interested in signing me on, they sent me 20 scripts to read. I called them to ask if there was money attached to this. In other words, if I liked one of the scripts, would I get an offer to direct it? They replied with, "No!" I asked, "Why I should read all of those scripts then?" That was the end of our relationship.

THE PROFANE EXHIBIT

Wannabe producer David Bond started to produce *The Profane Exhibit* (2013) around 2010. It was meant to be a violent compilation film where 8 to 10 directors contributed short horror films. I shot the episode "Basement in LA" at my own expense with Clint Howard, Tara Cardinal, and Chance Minter starring. Chance Minter was one of the critics I beat up in the boxing ring and is now a fledgling producer in LA. I built the set in the actual basement of a porn studio in the San Fernando Valley. My episode was supposed to reflect a day in the life of the Austrian murderer Fritzl who locked his daughter in the basement for 20 years, repeatedly raped her, and even got her pregnant several times. He killed the babies after they were born and kept his daughter in the basement.

The problem with *The Profane Exhibit* was that David Bond went broke, and the film never was finished until other producers took over. Over a decade later, the film came out in 2023 worldwide on DVD and Blu-ray. I never got paid for it.

IN THE NAME OF THE KING 3:
THE LAST MISSION

Since the DVD and TV sales of the first two In the Name of the King films were still going very well, it made sense to shoot a third entry for around $1.5 million. The second film cost almost $5 million. You can't make a cloak and dagger fantasy film like that in Canada for $1.5 million. I found a CGI investment partner from Pakistan, Ice Animation, who did the effects and made a much better CGI dragon than what we had in *In the Name of the King 2: Two Worlds*.

The Boyana studios in Sofia, Bulgaria made a great offer for us to shoot *In the Name of the King 3: The Last Mission* over there. Even though the company is owned by Avi Lerner from Millenium Films and Nu Image, I decided to go with them. We made a deal. They got all the props and costumes from *In the Name of the King: A Dungeon Siege Tale* that were stored in Germany. I was paying for the storage, but they could pick up the props in Germany at their own expense. In return, I got studio equipment, costumes, and props from *300: Rise of an Empire* (2014) and *Conan the Barbarian* (2011) for not that much money.

The crews in Bulgaria were significantly better than they were in Croatia or Romania. It also helped that Avi Lerner shot big action films with movie stars before in recent years (*The Expendables, The Black Dahlia* (2006)). Of course, those big Hollywood films have inflated budgets which work something like this… Stars are paid millions of dollars at act in the movies, but the filmmakers save money by only spending 1 or 2 million for the below-the-line production costs. A movie like *Killing Season* (2013) starring Robert De Niro and John Travolta could be sold as $25 million productions around the globe. Eventually, some were prosecuted for tax evasion in the US and money laundering in Bulgaria, but it didn't look like it hurt their careers all that much. They still own the studio, now run by Avi's son, and they still produce films. Similar to how it worked at Emmett / Furla Oasis Films, they hire big actors and spend less on below-the-line.

Dan Clarke managed the production again very well, but he hated the two women that the studio forced him to use as line producers. As always in former Eastern Communist countries, they still wanted to cheat us. We had to open a production company that would get the VAT back there which was supposed to be paid directly to me. In the end, they said that we had gone over budget despite this not being anywhere near the truth. l knew if I paid the last installment of money to the studio, they would still never pay me my VAT back a few months later, so I didn't make the final payment. I argued this could be offset against the VAT they owed me. Tatyana, who was also the girlfriend of the studio manager, freaked out. In the end, she had no choice. To this day, they're trying to get me to film in Bulgaria again.

We shot the medieval village at the studio lot. Action scenes were mostly shot in a forest and in a large cave. The climactic battle in a castle were shot around five hours away from Sofia. The locations all looked much better than the mini-fortress we built in the Canada for *In the Name of the King 2: Two Worlds*. The Bulgarian actors were very good, so we only had to fly in Dominic Purcell as the main actor. We stayed in the Kempinski Hotel for only 55 euros a night. Unfortunately, the hotel was not close to the inner city, so we had to take a taxi to the city center if we wanted to go out to a restaurant in our free time.

The food was not so good, just like in Romania and Croatia. Eventually, I found a small French bistro that was nice. Many times, I ate there alone just after the shoot. Nobody else from the crew was a foodie like me, so they ate fast food or went to the crappy restaurant in the hotel.

We had three six-day weeks with only Sundays off. Sofia is really an ugly Eastern city. A few times, Dominic and I walked from the hotel down to a small café to grab a slice of cake. Several bodyguards trained in the gym at the hotel, leaving their guns hanging in the locker room. I could have stolen their guns if I wanted to, but I decided against it because the bodyguards were clearly gangster types.

The shoot went well. *In the Name of the King 3: The Last Mission* turned out better than *In the Name of the King 2: Two Worlds*. With the worldwide collapse of DVDs and Blu-rays, the In the Name of the King film franchise was over. Later, we retooled In the Name of The King as a TV series for streamers, but nobody wanted it. That was a surprise for me because all three films did well around the world and were viewed by over 100 million people collectively. Overall, I would consider making films in Bulgaria again, but only if my money remained under strict control.

RAMPAGE: CAPITAL PUNISHMENT

About 5 years after making my first Rampage film, I began to wonder about the continued adventures of Bill Williamson. He ran away with the money after his killing spree, and, apparently got away with it. I got the best reviews of my career for *Rampage*. In Germany and the US, sales weren't bad. I asked Brendan Fletcher if he would take part in another one, and he enthusiastically agreed. I developed the idea for a sequel in which Bill has become more political and stayed connected to the world via YouTube, building up a fanbase.

In *Rampage: Capital Punishment*, he breaks into a TV station and takes hostages. He uses the hostages to blackmail the network into broadcasting a live interview with him in which he dismantles the real politics driving the Bush and Obama presidencies. The film was made in only seven days for around $600,000. I was able to convey all my frustrations about our planet through Bill's big speech at the end. We are destroying the world with our wrong politics. Politicians are the henchmen of the super-rich. Climate change, along with senseless wars and idiotic religion, will cause us to use up all our resources and end up in a Mad Max style post-apocalyptic future that will wipe out most of humanity.

We shot everything in Maple Ridge and built the TV studio in an old battery factory. My wife Natalie was the line producer, and she got the locations, crew, and actors for cheap. A lot of the crew was from my bigger movies and took pay cuts to just work with me again. Mathias shot every scene again with two or three RED cameras. Jonathan Shore was still helping with the post-production. The only regular crewmembers I could not use for this film were my line producers, Shawn Williamson and Dan Clarke, since they had become too expensive by now.

Natalie did a super job as my line producer. She was used to doing TV shows quickly and cheaply, but even she was very surprised at how quickly I was filming. Even with only seven days of filming, I didn't go over. Only equipped with a treatment, Brendan as Bill and Lochlyn Monroe as the TV reporter did a great job in particular. I played the TV station manager and did a really bad job of it. I had no choice. We didn't plan to have this as a speaking role, but then decided to give him some dialogue and no other actors were available except for me.

The shoot had a lot of action and explosions. If you are shooting a small film, it's wise to spend money on the big action scenes. You need to film fast with limited acting roles and not too many locations. Filmmaking means bargaining all the way through.

The German dubbing for *Rampage: Capital Punishment* was super good. When I screened with the film in German cinemas, I had great discussions with the audience about the film's political impact.

After *Rampage: Capital Punishment*, I didn't film anything for two years because the market for independent films got worse by the day. My company Event Films remained active in the market and sold films from other producers and directors worldwide, but this market was also in a downturn. For example, I bought the worldwide rights to KING COBRA (2016) starring James Franco and Christian Slater for $450,000. I was happy when the film's investor bought the rights back from me for $550,000. It was already difficult to get a total of $450,000 worth of investments from all over the world for a James Franco film.

I had 2 projects (The Viking and 12 Hours) that I wanted to shoot in Bulgaria, but the only way to make money with such genre films would be to shoot the whole film for around $1.5 million if a big star like Nicolas Cage, Bruce Willis or Kevin Costner played the lead role. I even made an offer to Cage for $800,000 for 3 weeks of shooting 6 days a week, but he refused. I was active in the film markets in Berlin, AFM, and Cannes.

We booked sales, but the sales results were worse and worse, so there was always a war going on inside me. I wanted to make films and tell stories, but I also wanted to be financially successful and not subsidize my business with my own savings. I missed being on the set because filming was always the best part of making movies for me. Since I wasn't directing films anymore, about 70% of my professional life took place behind my desk. I've answered hundreds of emails every day for the last two decades; these can vary from business letters to contracts to lawsuits and so on.

RAMPAGE: PRESIDENT DOWN

Somehow, I wasn't done with the film world yet. Every day, I was getting more and more frustrated every day about the political situation (ISIS, refugees, polar ice caps melting, rich people getting richer). Deep down, I also wasn't done with the story about Bill Williamson. Somehow the Rampage films have become my twisted take on the film *Boyhood* (2014) except we just don't follow a family over several years, but a mass murderer instead. Bill had gotten away with his massacres twice, and now I wanted to bring it to a realistic, but also disturbing and radical end. My thought is what if his wish came true… "We have to overthrow the government and kill the rich!"

Brendan Fletcher had just completed 88 days of filming on the Leonardo DiCaprio film *The Revenant*. He thought he was a big shot and wanted more money to play Bill again. My plan was to only pay him $5,000 with a plan to shoot again in just 6 days right at the start of January. It would be fast and cheap, but with a lot of action. I wanted to say goodbye to the BIG film industry with a bang.

Brendan flew to Washington, D.C. to shoot some B-roll for the film for a scene with Ari Taub. Taub, my line producer buddy from New York, had worked with me before on *Assault on Wall Street*, *Alone In The Dark 2* (2008) (which I produced but not directed), and my cigarette commercial for PALL MALL in NY in 2001. They shot second unit footage in front of the White House, the Senate, the Lincoln Memorial, and other famous places in DC.

Right before Christmas, Brendan's agent told me that he wanted $25,000 to play the lead in *Rampage: President Down* because he now was worth a lot more. What an outrage! Everyone worked for almost nothing, and I wouldn't earn a cent either. He wanted a producer and co-writer credit. I let his agent know I was extremely angry about all this, and Brandon had already agreed to reprise his role of Bill Williamson for the originally discussed fee of $5,000. If I had to pay him 25K, I would not greenlight the movie. I was in a tough spot. The locations and crew were already booked. Brendan had all the leverage. If he had told me $25,000 before, I wouldn't have sent him to Washington, D.C. in the first place. I threatened to sue him, and we agreed on $10,000. When I later watched *The Revenant*, I barely saw Brendan in it. He had been on set for maybe 80 days of filming, but he didn't even have five lines in the film. Hell, he wasn't even in the film for five minutes! What total bullshit!

My composer Jessica de Rooij, whose career I helped a lot by always hiring her, was now heavily involved in the German TV business and had two small children. I offered her 10,000 euros to compose the score for *Rampage: President Down*. She agreed to consult on the score instead. I booked a Canadian music producer for $2,000.

Before the actual filming, we filmed Bill's YouTube videos at my house. This is how I was able to shorten the main shoot to five days of filming. The filming started on January 2nd, 2016, in Jamestown, about an hour outside of Vancouver. We filmed for three days in a large forest and started with all the action scenes. We had over 50 explosions, 40 stunt people who flew through the air, and all the scenes set in the cave that Bill Williamson dug into the ground. The cave location was in Jamestown on the site and in an original railway tunnel that we only dressed. A lot of props came from my house: old bags, a grill, blankets, computers, and all the files that were on the tables in the FBI office. We had to save money where we could. It was cold when we were filming, but the frost on the ground made for some sensational images. You can see some on my website at http://bollfilms.com/.

Everything went wonderfully without any injuries, accidents or insurance claims. but some of our crew members were shit, and we had other problems. Wardrobe did a good job at first, but then lost control over continuity on police uniforms and even lost $2,500 worth of uniforms. Our production designer Vava said she had no idea what happened to them. Later, we realized she was trying to build the police office in a studio. We spent two days filming in the Maple Ridge film studios, right around the corner of the old bingo hall in the first Rampage movie, which is now bankrupt. Vava had to prepare a living room for Bill's girlfriend, an FBI office, and a TV studio. It quickly became clear she had never held a hammer or drilled a hole in her life, and her staff was also useless. We hired two carpenters overnight who finished everything as quickly as possible.

The only location that looked like shit was the TV studio, but we saved it because we shot the news anchors almost behind the scenes the whole time, which made it feel more like a documentary and was actually stronger for the film. One of the two news reporters was a Muslim, and he told me he had problems with the dialogue. I replied that my Rampage movies were meant to be satires. He already agreed to play the part, and I let him know he wasn't allowed to back out. I treated him very well but wondered why he accepted the role in the first place?

The actor who was the biggest problem on set was Steve Baran, who played one of the two FBI agents. He prepared extremely well for filming. We had the same political opinion as me, and he loved the *Rampage* films. Unfortunately, he couldn't improvise at all. He always tried to recite his memorized texts and could only do so too stiff and woodenly. I shot his scenes over and over again, letting the camera run for 20 minutes at a time. I shook them up a bit from the outside. Sometimes I played the colleague, sometimes the boss. I wanted the FBI boys to react like real FBI agents, but this was too difficult for them. While Brendan Fletcher was totally into it, the actors playing the cops had a hard time.

This day of filming took longer than normal because I wanted to get everything out of the actors. In between, I put them in the car and had them drive around in the car with Mathias, a camera, and me. Even these conversations hardly ended up in the final film.

As a surprise, I emailed the FBI agents on- camera video recordings of Brendan in the forest where he threatened the agents. These scenes were gold because the actors reacted to them in a more natural way. In the movie, Bill Williamson has a double agent in the FBI office who feeds him all the information and lets him hack into the computer system. Bill knows everything about the agents, making him one step ahead of them. When he threatens their families, they react believably. Of the 4 hours of material, only 20 minutes ended up in the film. Luckily, we shot a lot of material in the forest, so the film ended up being 90 minutes long. When you're filming for so few days, you're always afraid that there won't be enough material in the end.

Natalie line produced again, but she just had our son Walter. When she came home after a 15-hour day of filming to a baby that won't sleep, it made her fall sick and she became unfocused. The filming was also harder for me than normal because we also had to manage journalists, a documentary team from Germany, and several extras who had bought roles in the film through our successful crowdfunding campaigns. Working with extras who were also fans was challenging because they wanted to talk to me the whole time in the middle of a shoot! They were all very nice, though, which made it easier for me. I knew we only had a week of mayhem shooting this movie, and then it would all be in the can. I wouldn't have made it under those circumstances if the shoot was any longer; I would have gotten the flu or something.

At the time, I thought *Rampage: President Down* would be my last film. Kelvin, who edited *Rampage: Capital Punishment*, was there again and did a great job. We also bought original news footage again to make the film as realistic as possible. I already booked the dates for my last cinema tour in the summer 2016 in Germany, and I was very happy screening the film in around 10 cinemas.

Finished with filmmaking, I wondered what I'd do next. As a big foodie, I thought opening a restaurant would be a good idea!

BAUHAUS

My restaurant Bauhaus opened in Vancouver in 2015. I invested $2.2 million into the renovation and went $700,000 over budget. The Canadian craftsmen were complete failures, and, let's say, the landlord was not my friend. We ended up in an endless lawsuit in 2021 that got settled with no gain for either me or him. In commercial real estate, the landlord has the law on his side. I started to invest in Vancouver commercial buildings around this same time, but I'm a fair landlord to my tenants. Because the restaurant opened late in mid-May 2015, and I had already planned my summer in Germany from June 28th to September 5th, Natalie and I didn't feel particularly good about leaving Vancouver when it opened.

Stefan Hartmann, our first chef, was great. The manager Tim, who said he worked for the Queen of England, was an absolute failure and we fired him before we left to Germany. The new manager Donald turned out to be an alcoholic and was barely working, but we couldn't fire him while we were on vacation. In the restaurant business, you need to fire a manager in person and walk him off the premises or else your money and wine disappear. The bartender was also a cheat, and we also fired him when we returned from Germany. I filed criminal charges against both of them to no avail. In September 2015, Natalie became managing director of the restaurant and found Aga, who became our assistant manager. I went to the restaurant almost every evening to build up a personal relationship with the guests, which worked pretty well.

We sat 100 people in Bauhaus, which was an expensive high-end German restaurant. We built our reputation slow but steady. It was important for us to watch our staff and the kitchen every day. Social media Influencers (Twitter, Facebook, Instagram), food critics and hotel concierges had to be invited to help spread the word.

We also had to encourage companies to hold lunches and dinner at our restaurant. It was a slow grind. Many concierges told us that we were the best restaurant in Vancouver but would end up recommending other restaurants to people because they had known the owners for years and took bribes. Restaurant awards are often bought, and most of the Canadians have no idea about good food because of their British roots. There are now 20 good restaurants in Vancouver. Since 2022, 8 of these have even earned a prestigious Michelin star. Traditional British cuisine is just tasteless to me no matter if it's Beef Wellington, poutine, or the rest of the rubbish. In my opinion, not one restaurant in Vancouver is worthy of a Michelin star. In Europe, none of them would even qualify.

The problem for us was that food and alcohol in Canada are expensive to buy, costing about double what they would in Germany. Canada also has high taxes on alcohol. Running a restaurant is like shooting a film without an end in sight. It takes a lot of energy, but you have moments of success making guests happy and having regulars come back for meals. When it comes to films, everyone now says, "I liked your movie! I saw it for free on BitTorrent or YouTube."

As soon we went over every summer to Germany, the staff stole from us and poured a lot of free drinks for themselves and their friends. Running Bauhaus was a lot of hard work, and was a financial loss in the end. Even with 100 or 200K of profits a year, we were 10 years away from getting our opening costs of $2.2 million back. After five years, COVID-19 started and we had to close the restaurant.

Closing Bauhaus lined up with our moving to Germany in 2020 so our son Walter could start elementary school there. My son KJ was now old enough to stay more with his mother and only visit us on holidays. We visit him when we're back in Vancouver from time to time. My wife's daughter Angelina was going to try out a private English-speaking school in Cologne. The problem for both kids was that moving at the start of the COVID shutdown made it impossible for them to make friends at school.

Their first year in Germany was very lonely for them. After a year, Angelina moved back to Vancouver to live with her grandma and finish school there. She graduated in 2024. In Germany, Walter had to repeat second grade because he didn't learn German well due to the very bad online school system. In our household, I spoke German to Walter. As a whole, we speak more English in the house because Natalie's German is not good.

GERMANY DURING THE WINTER OF 2022

It's the winter of 2022. My book *Tabula Rasa* was almost complete.

After 17 years of arthritis and hobbling about, I got a new hip in the summer. I had gotten used to my pain, but it was getting worse over the years. My knees and left hip had osteoarthritis, so I had to get surgery to keep my other joints from being destroyed. At the Emma Clinic in Seligenstadt, I was treated by Dr. Manfred Krieger who operated with the AMIS method. This method approached the entire operation from the front with a 10-centimeter incision on the upper thigh. The muscles are pulled apart, and the surgeon is able to hammer a 13-centimeter implant through this gap. The wound is just glued, shut. After eight days, the plaster gets removed and everything is healed. After the operation, you can stand on your leg right away with your full weight on it. I used crutches for about eight days and was able to drive a car after only five.

The boring, dull arthritic pain disappeared after the operation. Slowly, the pain from the surgery disappeared as well. On the one hand, my full recovery was positive, but I know that my knees and other hip won't last until the end of my life either.

The Corona virus has changed a lot of our lives the past few years. It has even affected my view of life itself! I am convinced that in the last seven months, in addition to norovirus and three-week long-term bronchitis, I have also had omicron and either long COVID or post-vaccine symptoms. I have felt muscle twitching, tingling, the feeling of being under electricity, and a depressive phase after getting one of the vaccines. Over 60,000 people have now reported similar symptoms as well on the record. Although these symptoms subsided, the spring of 2022 was really shit, War in Ukraine had broken out and inflation and recession were getting out of control.

The depression felt like a hard lump down in my stomach. I had a constant feeling of excitement that wouldn't let me sleep. The antidepressant mirtazapine helped me to sleep right away, but after two weeks I started to feel very unpleasant hunger pangs. I replaced the medication with St. John's Wort (Jarsin, 900 mg per day), which helped me very well because it works in the same way as the anti-depressants as a serotonin inhibitor/regulator. After eight weeks, I stopped this too. The depressive phase didn't come back, even though there were countless reasons to continue to be depressed.

The "being underpowered" symptoms were by no means over, and my muscles were twitching. Somehow, I knew I wasn't the same, I wasn't symptom-free, and I kept thinking about the aging process and death, which was getting ever closer.

The fact that death is an inevitability is a shitty feeling. I now feel deep inside that I might not die at an old age like my parents, but instead I will die younger than them. That makes me nervous and also angry because there is no reason or diagnosis for my imminent demise. If something changes permanently in the body, then you must try to get to the bottom of the matter. I had my doctors run an MRI of my abdomen and do some blood tests. All they showed was that I have high cholesterol levels and need to take statins again, but otherwise I don't have any abnormal values that fall into the catastrophic levels. An MRI of my head also ruled out that I had ALS, Alzheimer's or a brain tumor. Blood sugar, liver and kidney values were in the upper range but still within normal limits. Daily breathing exercises using the Wim Hof Method and cold showers help me a lot because they make you feel stronger and more relaxed. Just read the book *The Wim Hof Method: Activate Your Full Human Potential*, it's completely worth your time.

Nevertheless, the helplessness that remained was new for me. The combination of the end of the world (Ukraine, climate change, the collapse of the West and democracy), my not very active film director career, and the fact that my brother doesn't talk to me anymore or want to do anything with me anymore doesn't help either.

From 2013 to 2020, I lived in Canada more than in Germany. I spoke to my brother Stefan almost every day via WhatsApp. We exchanged information about world politics and our personal lives. Later in 2020, my wife Natalie and I moved permanently to Mainz and started our son Walter in 1st grade. At the time, Walter spoke mostly English and very little German. His first school year was a disaster because of Corona and the required school closures made remote learning the new standard. By the time he reached the 3rd grade, he was so behind in reading and writing that we have decided to have him take 2nd grade over again to catch up on basics of German.

During the Corona pandemic, my brother developed into an overly cautious isolationist who did not tolerate any visitors. He even asked his children to take daily rapid tests. Even though I lived closer to him now than I had in years, we only had contact through WhatsApp again. His girlfriend was allowed to see him in person, but ultimately nobody else was.

In 2021, the COVID-19 vaccination was finally widely available in Germany. Since our family doctor in Burscheid had enough vaccines, he vaccinated my brother and me in the spring of 2021. Since I was now vaccinated, I went to my visit my brother and stayed over there for the night after passing a quick test. A day trip there didn't make sense because the distance from Burscheid to Mainz is around 180 km. We rode bikes and ate meals together. It felt like old times. We also visited my parents' grave in the Odenthal Mourning Forest.

Three months later, I was allowed to come back after getting the second vaccine. Everything went just as well as the first time. After that second visit, I haven't seen him since. He told me that I was stressing him out and cut off contact completely without a good reason.

My brother had done this once before when he was married, and then apologized to me years later. At that time, I was standing in front of his door on Christmas Eve with my mother and my two dogs, Daisy and Laura. Out of nowhere, he didn't want to let the dogs in his house anymore. The dogs had been with him dozens of times before, and he even had a dog himself. I assume the real reason was his wife at the time hated me and didn't want me there on Christmas Eve. My mother and I went back to my parents' apartment and spent the evening with my father. As always, my father was in a bad mood and shared his herring salad with us.

The real absurdity of this situation struck me on December 24th. It didn't matter to me that my brother told me that my dogs weren't allowed in because he tried everything to keep his wife from getting upset, but he didn't succeed. His marriage was fucked up. She didn't love him anymore and had other lovers. About two years later, he threw her out and after a few months, he normalized his relationship with me. From then on, we spent a lot of time together when I was in Germany. He also came to Mainz regularly and helped me with the gardening. He even flew over to Vancouver to visit me twice.

Our second break in contact in 2021 hit me harder because I loved visiting my hometown and spending time with my brother. At the same time, I was also able to visit other friends and my tax advisor. That was all over now. I even had to stay overnight in a hotel in Cologne when I had appointments with TV production companies. This had never happened before in my life, and it really pissed me off. I spoke to him regularly on his WhatsApp account or emailed him, sending friends to check on how he was doing, but all I got were robot--like replies along the lines of, "Happy Holidays!"

I ended up telling my brother about my depression. I told him that whatever had happened was in the past, and we should have a regular relationship as brothers once more. He simply replied with, "You're fine with me. Go get professional help!"

Finally, I found out through my friend Hanno that my brother said I no longer played a role in my brother's life because he felt I always treated him like a servant. This clear statement helped me to be a little less sad and allowed me to analyze the situation. For example, if he felt that way because he brought me back and forth from the airport a few times a year, that's a real shame. I would have liked to have known about it earlier, because then I would have organized these trips a little differently. In recent decades, he has worked less and less for television and took a part-time position teaching in a special school in Cologne. He never got out of Burscheid and complained about this age.

We hired a Polish helper for my parents who initially only cleaned and cooked. In later years, she bathed my mother and changed her adult diapers. My father died in the hospital after falling down the stairs and breaking his femur. At first, everything looked good after the operation. Unfortunately, what killed him was the germs at the hospital. This is a common cause of death of older people and happens far too often. My mother became more and more demented and died peacefully in her sleep about two years after my father had passed.

I was not present for either of their deaths as I was living in Canada at the time, but I flew in for their funerals. My brother took care of everything for my parents both before and after their death: arranging the funeral, clearing out the apartment, fixing it up, and running it as a new rental property. To show him my appreciation for all the work he did for our parents, I often paid for our meals and drank the best wines with him. When he visited Canada, I was happy to pay for all of his expenses. My Golf GTI was available to him free of charge in Germany for almost an entire year.

After our parents died, it was a given for me that I would give up my share of the inheritance completely, meaning he could keep my parents' savings and completely take over the house in Burscheid with its six residential units. He had bought out our cousins' share of their house a long time ago. In the end, I gave him my share, which amounted to two apartments. It should also be mentioned that he lived in Grandma Hertha's house for ages. He took over her house for a bargain after her death. I only received 60,000 marks, and my father 120,000. The house was now worth around 400,000 euros. Nevertheless, he seemed to believe that I still owed him something.

In February 2021, shortly before we got vaccinated, he asked if I could give him around 200,000 euros to allow him to stop working as a teacher and enjoy an early retirement. I found this question to be incredibly impertinent because I have worked hard to earn my money and have defended my right to do so under unspeakable stress over my entire professional career. I told him he could sell his house, pocket at least 600,000 euros, pay off the loans, and still have 300,000 euros in net profit left over for himself.

Shortly after this phone call, nothing more came from him. When I visited him after I got vaccinated, it was already clear to him that these would be our final visits. I suspected that his current girlfriend might have been behind all this, thinking she might have said something like, "Uwe is rich and never took care of your parents. You were always there for her and sacrificed yourself. He owes you!"

It shocks me that he has no desire at all to talk and hang out with me. He always gave the impression that he loved my children and our dog Bessy. Walter always asks where his Uncle Stefan is. It seems that, just like in his marriage, he is centering his whole life on just one person and is not interested in maintaining his circle of family and friends. At the same time as me, he has also lost contact with all his relatives and friends, only answering them like a robot and no longer allows meetings in-person. I would be happy to have him in my life again, and I would probably be ready to forget about this whole thing and put it behind us. It's not my fault he never made it out of Burscheid.

In the summer of 2022, after more than two years of the pandemic, I was not in good mental and physical shape. Many of my friends were the same way. In addition to the shutdowns and restrictions on our lives, a lot of our joy for life had also been destroyed.

Despite triple vaccination, most people got Corona anyway. Many even got it multiple times. Unfortunately, the vaccine often had negative side effects which only lasted around three months. I felt the vaccine only prevented severe cases of Corona. In over 99% of cases, Omicron is like a moderate flu and is not fatal whether one is vaccinated or not.

We will have to live with the fact that COVID, like the flu, will continue to mutate and that we may get it every year. That doesn't exactly make us happy, but what really weighs us down is bigger issues like the Ukraine war and the associated inflation, recession, and the fear of World War III with the inevitable deaths as a result. Europe and the US will become weaker. Dictatorships like China and Russia will win. In the EU, states such as Sweden, Italy, Poland and Hungary are already governed by far right-wing parties.

There is a great danger that Donald Trump or another ego-driven corrupt candidate will win the election for president in the US in 2024 or 2028. If that happens, then the US will no longer be a democracy. NATO and the EU will collapse. In France, Macron is no longer allowed to run in the next election. In their most recent election, only 20% of the total population voted for him. Even worse, 40% of the population in both France and Italy has stopped voting at all. As soon as the radical parties get their turn in France, the EU will be history because both Marine Le Pen and the Communists want to get out.

At any rate, it is crystal clear that the extreme left and extreme right parties are moving closer together and will probably form coalitions with each other more often in the future. The climate crisis is already causing enough trouble in the world. Forecasts for the future were already catastrophically bad, but the war and the disintegration of democracy make me think that neither my children nor myself will die of old age. In previous years, we discussed people's stupidity, but we weren't really afraid that our lives would fall apart completely.

Now, the real fear of such things is there for me. I can hardly really be happy about anything any longer. Living in the moment and being content is becoming increasingly difficult. The shadow of total despair and the actual end of our civil society hovers over everything. It could be that everything here will be bombed, or a fascist election or revolution will plunge Europe into dictatorships. We will have no electricity and have nothing to eat. The soil shall become too dry. Other parts of the world will be flooded. I expect all this will happen within the next 15 years. We don't even need to talk about the situation in third-world countries because hundreds of millions will die miserably even without there being another world war.

I wrote extensively about the making of my films in my book *Ihr könnt mich mal!* so I won't repeat everything here. Nevertheless, I want to draw a line between the time when I wrote most of *Tabula Rasa* and now. Thus far, this book has made readers very aware of my youth, studies and early professional years. Without my first paid jobs at WestCom and Taunus Film GmbH, my film career would probably have been different or not happened at all. After *German Fried Movie, Barschel: A Murder in Geneva*, and *Amoklauf*, my film career would have been over. I would have become a teacher or a journalist who would have continued to try to make films all his life. Without the required film funding or TV money, the only things I could have made would have been cheap amateur films. Make no mistake, these two companies made *The First Semester* possible. My later international films were possible thanks to Taunus Film turning to film funds.

Between 2000 and 2015, I directed the following feature films starring many world famous stars: *Sanctimony, Blackwoods, Heart of America, House of the Dead, Alone in the Dark, BloodRayne, In the Name of the King: A Dungeon Siege Tale, Seed, Postal, BloodRayne 2: Deliverance, Far Cry, 1968 Tunnel Rats, Stoic, Rampage, Attack on Darfur, The Final Storm, Max Schmeling, BloodRayne: The*

Third Reich, Blubberella, Auschwitz, In the Name of the King 2: Two Worlds, Suddenly, In the Name of the King 3: The Last Mission, Rampage: Capital Punishment, and *Rampage: President Down.* During this time, I produced some films I did not direct including *House of the Dead 2* (2005), *Alone in the Dark 2, Zombie Massacre* (2013), and *Zombie Massacre 2: Reich of the Dead* (2015). All in all, I did 26 films as a director and producer in this 14-year timespan and have made a grand total of 37 films as a director to date.

At the same time, I opened Boll AG in Germany and Event Film Distribution in Canada, which was responsible for selling all of these films internationally. My relationship with Christine at the time became more and more of a long-distance relationship. After *In the Name of the King: A Dungeon Siege Tale* wrapped, it ended. My first marriage, which included to the birth of my first son KJ developed during the *Postal* shoot. To be frank, it also had no real chance of survival and fell apart within four years. The reason why I stayed almost exclusively in Canada between 2013 and 2020 was less because of my films than it was to be closer to my son. I wanted to be a good father, so I had split custody and lived nearby.

During this time, I also met and married my second wife and had my second son. This marriage lasts to this day! Even though my wife is Canadian, she thought it was a good idea to move to Germany in 2020. After all these films and credits, I thought that this time around I'd have better luck in my home country with the broadcasters, film funding agencies, and the streamers like Netflix, Sky, and Amazon. I decided to develop projects for the German market and have them financed through the typical German method of TV plus film subsidies. This results in no intrinsic risk, which is the same method Danny Levy, Leander Haußmann, Wim Wenders, and all other German directors have done it their whole career

I immediately got to work with my old friend and business partner Michael Roesch from Kinostar Filmverleih. In the documentation area, we created a pitch for a documentary about the Bandidos

MC. Through my friend Ralf Seeger, I got to know the heads of the German Bandidos, who have had to deal with bans on vests and clubs for several years. They were currently on trial in Hagen for, among other things, forming a criminal organization. At first Netflix and Amazon were enthusiastic, but then became afraid and worried for their safety.

The large company Banijay Group (*Germany Is Searching The Superstar*, *Who Wants To Be A Millionaire?*), had entered the documentary sector in 2021. They told me they would finance the documentary. So, whenever I wanted to film a Bandidos event (rocker parties, meetings, court proceedings, etc.), they would send me a film crew. In mid-2022, Banijay walked out of the project because they couldn't find a buyer for the film, leaving me to finish the documentary alone.

ARD, ZDF, and all the private broadcasters and streamers canceled our big historical series in development, *Captain Veit* and *In The Name Of The King* even though the latter was already well known thanks to my film trilogy. ARD Degeto Film at least gave us detailed reasons for the cancellations, but ZDF and the rest gave us no feedback. We continued with pitches for four documentaries and six films. Since there is a high turnover at Netflix, you can often end up resubmitting the same projects after a few months because the managers will be all new at this time. We've introduced *Bandidos* to Netflix four times in two years; each time, no one had any idea about was the project was about.

I tend to watch a lot of Netflix and other streaming channels. They show a lot of documentaries. Of course, my *Bandidos* documentary would definitely have high viewer ratings. So, after a year of trying to get films and TV shows going, the suspicion arose in my mind that nobody wanted to work with me. I was still blacklisted and would never get a foothold in German filmmaking.

HANAU

The German film that I really wanted to score points with for my filmmaking comeback was *Germany In Winter*, a dystopia that shows what Germany will be like in ten years. The story begins with the AFD or some similar right-wing party having taken over Germany. We follow two police officers who murder asylum seekers with the knowledge and support of the new Interior Minister. A journalist who reports on this story ends up being murdered.

I managed to get Axel Milberg and Max Riemelt to agree to play the main roles. Roesch and I submitted funding applications in Baden-Württemberg, and the managing director supported the application, but the jury rejected it 8-0. The jury consists of four SWR editors and four artists and/or state officials. Their verdict was that my scenario was too harsh and too radical.

Months later, the same funding round also rejected script funding for *Captain Veit* despite the fact that the writers Michael Roesch and Peter Scheerer from Kinostar are from Stuttgart and the story takes place during the Peasants' Wars in Baden-Württemberg. The funding management wanted to approve the money for this project too, but just like with *Germany in Winter*, it was rejected by the jury again. This is another prime example of how TV broadcasters usually steal subsidies for their TV co-productions.

Kai Finke from Netflix told me the script for *Germany In Winter* was incredibly powerful, but that he can no longer decide to make it because he had moved over to series co-productions. His successor canceled my project within 24 hours. Before her Netflix job, she worked at Neue Constantin Film. Amazon and all other broadcasters I submitted the project to also denied funding a short time later.

I wasn't prepared to pay for the film in full myself, so I put the project on hold for the time being. I definitely wanted to shoot something political. I came up with a scenario for *Hanau* (2022) based on the real mass-shooting that took place in the city of Hanau on February 19th, 2020. This shooting that left 11 dead was the first QAnon mass murder in Germany. The attacker had left behind a manifesto that was over 30 pages long and proved he had clearly been radicalized by conspiracy theories on the Internet.

I had already made many several films about AMOK RUNS and shootings with *Amoklauf, Heart Of America, Rampage, Rampage: Capital Punishment, Rampage: President Down*, and *Assault on Wall Street*. I'm also an expert on the topic of violence escalations with my movies *Attack On Darfur, Auschwitz, Stoic*, and *Postal*. I gathered crew and cast members for cheap and decided to shoot the film in my hometown of Mainz. Steffen Mennekes, with whom I had already worked with in *Stoic*, another one of my films based on a real-life murder, was exactly the right person for such an intense role. He looked like the son-in-law that mothers want but had no problems moving over into the deep psychological abyss.

The victims' families did not want to meet me and showed no interest in a feature film on the subject. I would have liked to have conducted interviews with the survivors and the victims' families in order to put a documentary on the DVD and incorporate further research into my script from first-hand sources. Of course, I had researched all the existing documentation, articles and published files on the rampage and perpetrators. I wanted to make a film from the perpetrator's perspective the whole way through. I drove around Hanau and looked at the crime scenes to get a solid spatial sense of what was going on. I looked for similar locations in Mainz. We shot the film within two weeks in February 2021. Post-production took over six months as I tried out many cuts before finally mastering the film.

As soon as the film was announced, a public shit storm followed. The press acted like UWE BOLL and ONLY UWE BOLL is not allowed to make a film about real tragedies. They wrote that I didn't ask the families for their input and didn't care about the victims. That's not accurate at all! The victims' families sued the government and the police, accusing them of not stopping the killer when he went to shoot up a hookah lounge and a kiosk. They wanted to get a lot of money from the state, and didn't like that my film showed that the police could not stop the shooter because everything happened so fast.

After his first massacre at the hookah bar, the murderer drove off just three minutes later. One guy followed him to the kiosk. When the shooter stopped there, he first turned around and shot the guy that was following him through his windshield. He then entered the kiosk and killed another four people. A mere two minutes later, he drove home and killed his mother and himself. He was a very good shooter and acted fast. The police had no time in which to stop him.

Where I think the police failed was that the shooter was known in the little town as a kind of crazy guy who was under psychologist treatment. The police knew of stories he was telling people that the CIA had put a computer chip in him when he was a baby. Despite all this, they still let him keep his guns, which was a deadly mistake. He would never have been able to commit mass murder if he didn't have the guns to begin with. My film gave everybody the facts, and neither side liked them.

Hanau was finished and released on physical media and streamers around a year after filming ended in March 2022. The film was not a financial success. The only real review written about it was very positive. Only Scandinavia bought the film outside of Germany. We released it on Amazon Prime and Apple TV on our own.

FIRST SHIFT

Based on my negative experience shooting *Hanau*, my first film shot in Germany in decades, I decided to make international films again since there is practically no market for German genre films anymore. Only dramas and romantic comedies get film funding or TV orders, and I would get nothing in the end anyway. That's why I need to make films in the English language for an American audience starring world-famous actors. Without that, you will not sell a film anywhere!

First, I revived my older script *12 Hours* and wanted it rewritten to take place in South Africa. I had worked with Chris Roland, a South African producer, back when I filmed Attack on Darfur and 1968 Tunnel Rats. Roland did a pass on the script.

In *12 Hours*, a family man must kill 5 people in 12 hours to save his kidnapped family. I started casting the lead role through a casting agency in Los Angeles. Despite making very good offers, no star took the role. We offered $1.5 million for James McAvoy, Orlando Bloom, and Kit Harington to play the lead, but every one of them said no. By December 2022, we were in a bad situation. I would have to either cancel or postpone the film.

Despite all this, I really wanted to make a film again for an American audience. I had loved my past shoots in New York. I knew a line producer there, Ari Taub, who had organized a commercial shoot for Pall Mall early in my career; he also handled the New York scenes for *Assault on Wall Street* and *Alone in the Dark 2*. Taub agreed to organize a feature film shoot for me in March 2023.

I wrote *First Shift* (2024), which describes the first day of work for Deo and Angela, two police officers in Brooklyn. Deo prefers to work alone, but he gets assigned a new partner named Angela. The two of them experience a lot on their first shift! They rescue a dog, become involved in mafia murders, and witness a stabbing. Angela experiences a family tragedy involving her drug-addicted brother. There is something to laugh about, something to cry about, and pure excitement. I felt this was a good mix. Since I love police dramas, I was fully motivated to make a real comeback with this film.

I would only take my faithful cameraman Mathias Neumann with me, and then take use the rest of the crew from New York. Ari started on pre-production. We had hour-long Zoom calls talking about all the locations, crew members and shooting schedules. Location scouts fanned out and sent photos of possible filming locations such as the police headquarters, restaurants, and so on. We rejected many suggestions for crew members because they didn't have enough experience. It turned out that good crew members in New York are 30% more expensive than in Vancouver or Germany, so we ended up booking Axel and Lorenz, two cameramen from Germany. Patrick Grzanna and another cameraman also flew in to shoot a making-of documentary on *First Shift* and a documentary about me. As it turns out, these Germans would be saving our asses in short order.

In the beginning, everything still looked good. In January and February of 2023, we found all the filming locations and crew members as well as many experienced and well-known US actors. Kristen Renton plays Angela. She is best known as the female lead in *Sons Of Anarchy*. Gino Anthony Pesi, who starred in the TV series *Shades Of Blue* with Jennifer Lopez, was the first actor I hired because he understood the script thoroughly and was highly motivated. I offered little money to everyone, but since the script was well received, the New York casting agents Greer and Bowman managed to get bigger names even for smaller roles. Gary Pastore had experience playing mafiosos in 10 of Martin Scorsese's films. He also played a leading role in *The Deuce* with James Franco. Daniel Sauli had great experience on popular series like *The Blacklist* and *House Of Cards*. James McMenamin (*Manifest, Orange Is The*

New Black) and Willie C. Carpenter (*Gotham, Blue Bloods*) rounded out the cast.

That's one great thing about shooting in New York... A lot of very good actors live there. If you shoot on location, you can get these actors much cheaper than if you wanted to bring fly them to over to Vancouver or somewhere else.

Of course, the filming locations are also amazing even if New York is one of the most popular cities to film in along with Vancouver and Toronto. Since First Shift is practically a road movie, we wanted to shoot everything on location. We wanted to show the real New York with its 20 million people, the dirt, the chaos, but also the character of the city itself. We booked locations in Long Island, Staten Island, Brooklyn, Manhattan, and Queens.

At the end of February 2023, Mathias and I flew to New York to meet the crew, inspect all the filming locations, and run through the script with everyone. I met the actors for rehearsals and filming started a week later. We all lived in the Brooklyn neighborhood in Williamsburg. Mathias wanted an apartment, but I booked a room in Hotel 42 instead. While this was close to the production offices, it also was right next to the train and in the middle of Williamsburg. You could either hear the train or police sirens at all times.

In Williamsburg, there are a lot of blacks, Latinos and Orthodox Jews who have lived there forever. The latter are all dressed in black, wear fur hats and have curls of hair that hang down in a twisted manner. The women are not allowed to use contraception and wear wigs because they must shave their heads, and the children are dressed the same as the adults. It is an insular religious community that seems completely out of place. I was told the men study ancient scriptures all the time and don't work, but the women work. Still, I saw thousands of women with their strollers during the day, and the men were on their phones the whole time. I often walked past a wine shop filled with the men. Apparently, drinking is allowed.

Before filming, I invited Ari to the three-star restaurant Chef's Table Brooklyn Fare, which is in the back room of a supermarket. It's very expensive. It's one of those places where if you don't get there on time, the table will be fully charged to your credit card, and the table will be gone. I tell Ari this in advance, but he still picks me up way too late and then drives off to the restaurant in Manhattan. We almost hit cyclists several times, but it was almost their own fault because they also rode around like idiots. Every car in New York is driving around like crazy, and the streets are pure chaos. Cars often simply park on the street by the parking lane for hours, blocking the neatly parked cars. There are also tons of super-fast mini mopeds driving around everywhere, and nobody rides with a helmet like they should in the first place!

We can't get a parking space in front of the restaurant, so Ari parks directly in a no-parking zone, opens the hood and we go into the restaurant. After two and a half hours, our car was still there. We didn't get a ticket and weren't towed. He says that when a car has its hood up, nobody knows what to do and they leave it alone. We did the same thing again during our stay, and it worked again. During a location scout, a traffic police officer blocked an intersection. Ari showed him a police badge and told him that we have to turn left even though it's closed. The police officer waved us through. I couldn't believe any of Ari's tricks worked.

The first day of shooting was a complex one because we shot the beginning of the film in the police headquarters with dozens of extras. That day, Deo gets assigned his new partner Angela and isn't exactly thrilled about it. The production designer Anthony did a good job, and everything went well. I noticed that some crew members were at the junior level, but after 10 hours everything was done with the first day successfully completed.

Not only was Ari the line producer on the film, but he also had a costume and prop rental company from which we rented uniforms, police badges and weapons. On the third day, he was at lunch playing around with one of his rubber guns. This was seen by some crew members who made a huge scandal out of it. Since Alec Baldwin had recently shot his DP Halyna Hutchins in 2021 by accident on the set of his new Western film *Rust (2024)*, everybody on sets now panics whenever a weapon is used. The crew demanded that Ari be banned from the set. I thought it would be wisest to give in to the crew's demands since I wouldn't need him on set anyway; he could do more work for me in the production office anyway. The very next day, it became clearer that the crew just wanted to turn a mouse into an elephant. They now had a reason to involve the IATSE union and requested the entire production be carried out under union contracts going forward according to their rules. Among other things, this meant pension entitlements, more money for overtime, and a ton of bureaucracy. The union then contacted Ari and requested that he initially accept the union's offer as a negotiator. He rejected their offer. Most of the crew was determined to "flip the production" to a union one, even if they all agreed and signed a non-union contract in the first place. Our day rate for them was above the union minimums, so they had no reason to be unhappy. Ari and his partner Anthony told me that that signing with the union would cost me an extra $150,000 at least.

This situation on set boiled up on day four because the gaffer and the script girl were egging everyone on. They were no longer concentrating on the shoot at all and were openly talking about a strike if we didn't sign. They were fake-friendly to my face but disrupted the shoot and the performance of all the other employees. Above all, they were disrupting my concentration. The two leads, Kristen and Gino, were also pissed at the crew. The actual film began to suffer because of this. I asked Ari over the phone if we could get replacements if over 20 crew members didn't show up on set tomorrow, and he and Anthony confirmed they could.

The script girl sat next to me the whole time while we were shooting, looked right at me, and said, "I don't want to shut down your movie!" I replied with, "We will not sign with IATSE!" Their behavior implied that if we didn't kneel down and do what these motherfuckers wanted, there would be no more filming tomorrow.

At lunch, I told the gaffer and the script girl that they were responsible for this revolt, weren't concentrating on the work, and being irresponsible. She then completely freaked out and yelled at me claiming that I was a shitty director and that she was ten times better at it than me. There were witnesses to all of these conversations. I remained objective, but, of course, I fired her. She yelled at me more, insisting that I couldn't fire her. Five minutes later, she packed up her stuff and left. The gaffer was also fired by Ari two hours later.

We made it clear to the rest of the crew that they had valid contracts, and that if they didn't come to work the next day, it would be a breach of contract. If they insisted before filming that they would only take part in the film if we signed union contracts with them, then they would not have been hired in the first place. If we knew about this ahead of time, maybe we could have taken it into account beforehand. Most of my films have been union films, and I've never had a situation like this one on *First Shift*.

It looked like a war broke out just one day before my most expensive day of filming. The IATSE wrote to Ari that it had called on its members to strike, and that no one would be allowed to continue working on *First Shift*. They also said that our German cameramen were working on the set illegally and contacted the immigration authorities. Feeling queasy, I tried to at least get some sleep.

The next morning, my big mafia scenes were on the schedule. First, a drug dealer was interrogated and killed by two mobsters in an apartment. Afterwards, the two get interrogated and then shot on a high-rise roof. We had 10 actors on the clock, including Daniel Sauli, Gary Pastore and Aron Berg, all of whom were not cheap. Given that these were action scenes, there were also special effects and weapons to deal with.

When I woke up and drove to the set, calls were already coming in that protesters were standing in front of the set with signs and were trying to prevent actors and crew from entering the building. Now, the costume designers and camera assistants also wanted to strike. My actors were getting worried.

Somehow, I felt like I was back in my old *German Fried Movie* days when we were filming rogue on the run. Frank Lustig and I did almost all the camera shots for that film all those decades ago. As soon I came to the set of *First Shift*, I jumped out of my car and went to the truck with the costumes. I rolled the costume rack into the building with help from one of our drivers. The drivers remained loyal to us, as did police officer Tony Flynn who provided the locations. The protesters didn't dare speak to me. All of our German crew went inside followed by the actors. It was now important that our weapons expert and stunt coordinator didn't go on strike because that would have ended our day right then and there. Both came to the set and didn't give two shits about the strike.

The old saying "In danger and dire need, the middle path brings death!" still applies. It was clear to me that I had to go through with the entire day of filming, even though we were about three hours late and there were no lighting technicians, grips, digital image technician, make-up designers, costume designers, prop master, and so forth. In the end, you need a script, actors, sound, and camera to shoot, nothing more. I rehearsed with the actors while Mathias and his crew organized themselves. Leif, the cameraman on the documentary about me, became the focus puller on the A-camera. The problem was that we had no sound guy, but Ari was able to bring a Rastafarian from Jamaica who smelled so much of pot that it felt like we were in the middle of *Cheech and Chong's Next Movie* (1980).

We shot in Cinemascope with the Arri Alexa in 5K with two cameras, which retail for 300,000 euros apiece. Our camera package rental cost $40,000 for the film, but these cameras provided fantastic image quality. If the Germans wouldn't have been on the set that day, my film would have been canceled or I would have been forced to sign with IATSE.

I shot all of the scenes for the day in six hours. It helped that the Alexa is so sensitive to light that you can shoot in rooms with no extra lights and achieve very good results.

There were also demonstrations in front of the set the second day after the strike call, but by the third day the union was no longer interested so protests decreased. Ari and I were attacked by bitter crew members on Twitter and Instagram because they saw that they were now out of a job and production was continuing. PETA contacted me and said they had received an anonymous email saying we were treating a dog badly on set. Gino's dog in the film had a great time on set and was pampered and loved by everyone. Gino and Kristen, who owned three dogs at home just like me, had often supported PETA with donations. They wrote to PETA explaining the situation, and the issue was settled.

In one disturbing scene in the film, a family man kills his wife and stepson. The actors' union received an anonymous call that we were traumatizing a child on set and came to check. Some crew members did everything in their power to harm us. The labor board launched an investigation into whether workplace safety and standards were met. After about a week, the crew members began to claim that they had been fired, and wanted their full fees paid. In fact, no one was fired. Instead, the crew broke their contracts with us and stopped showing up for filming. What pathetic assholes! Talk about sneaky and self-deceptive losers.

The idea was that we would shoot a great film in New York in a relaxed atmosphere. Now, we were under a lot of stress filming to the old motto "Let's see whether we can continue filming or not tomorrow."

The law is that you can work in the US with a tourist visa as long as you are paid by an employer based in another country. This was exactly what we were doing! The Germans were paid by my company in Germany, and some were not paid at all because they were just helping their friends out. Others had green cards, like my old partner Michael Roesch. Patrick and Leif pitched in wherever something needed to be done to replace the crew. Ari and Anthony were nervous wrecks and couldn't get anything sorted for the last few days. Nevertheless, we continued filming with our skeleton crew. I was my own assistant director, production manager, and costume controller.

Gino and Kristen simply took their costumes with them to the hotel so they could come to the set already dressed. The film takes place in one day, so they had to wear just one costume the whole time.

On the last day of filming, we filmed a scene with Willie C. Carpenter where he gets his dog back from police officer Deo (Gino Pesi). We had booked a drone cameraman for to get the shot we wanted. Mathias had the idea that the drone guy with the camera should fly out of the park high above the East River and that our civilian police car would drive over the bridge with the drone flying parallel to it. Ari wanted to drive this car and was supposed to let us know via walkie-talkie once he was on the bridge. Of course, this being New York City, there was a traffic jam. It took quite some time for the car to arrive.

Meanwhile, I continued filming with the actors. I heard police sirens and Ari on the radio. He simply turned on the siren and tried to get over the bridge faster. All of a sudden, I heard more police sirens because the real cops were now stopping his car and asking him over the loudspeaker who he was and what he was doing. He yelled some bullshit back about how he had to make sure everything was all right without any further justification. Nevertheless, the cops drove on and basically let him go. I can hardly imagine that the police in Germany would let someone imitate a police officer in a fake police car and drive over a bridge with their lights flashing!

I followed up with the drone pilot to check if he had filmed everything. He said he lost his drone. I asked him what he meant, and I quickly realized that the drone had crashed. The footage was in the drone and totally lost. His $6,000 drone fell in the East River. Luckily, he accepted that he was at fault, and his insurance would cover the damage.

Another highlight of the ineptitude we encountered involved the props on set. We had a scene in a diner where Deo and Angela were having lunch with the police chief. The script said she was eating burgers. We shot the first take which didn't work out so well. We were getting ready to do a second take when it turned out that the prop guy had only prepared two burgers. No new food was available! Everyone who has worked on films knows that scenes are shot more than once. Enough food has to be prepared for several takes! We ended up filming the actors eating half-eaten burgers with more close-ups so the burgers looked like new.

Unfortunately, this wasn't the end of the story because the props guy wasn't a fast learner. Two days later, we shot a scene where Deo was supposed to eat a bagel. This time, the props boss had two bagels with him, so an 100% increase from last time. I sent him to Starbucks to buy more bagels like he should have had in the first place even though this added an unnecessary delay. I had previously told him to always have at least eight items of food if we were shooting a scene where people were eating. Even non-professionals should understand something like this as simply common sense.

In another scene, the script states that 15 kilos of drugs are found in a car. On the set, I was given a bag with six pills in it. I asked the new prop guy, who was just as stupid as the old one, if he had accidentally looked at the script at some point. I sent him to the grocery store to simply buy flour and sugar and put it in zip locks. He still only came back with 200 grams worth 3 dollars.

What I unfortunately learned from this crew is that today's generation no longer has any common sense. Instead, they have stupidity, ignorance, envy, resentment, laziness, and, worst of all, absolute entitlement. They believe iPhones, Frappuccinos, money, and other creature comforts are human rights regardless of whether they are at work or not.

Marijuana is now available everywhere in NY, and you can tell by the smell! Everyone smokes all day and is high, even our drivers! Michael Roesch was in a VW van. The driver suddenly couldn't find the hotels and drove in circles for twenty minutes, ending back up at the studio. Our driver couldn't find my hotel every morning without his navigation system even though he drove the same route every damn morning.

Ari organized a wrap party and even printed t-shirts for it. I told him that after all this shit we had to go through, I didn't feel like partying anymore and the crew didn't deserve it either. I stayed away from the party and invited Patrick and Leif to Peter Luger Steak House instead.

Afterwards, I went with Mathias to a comedy club in Manhattan to see our friend Aaron Berg (*Detroit Rock City* (1999)) there. Unfortunately, all the comedians before him were disastrous and boring woke shitheads, so we left before Aaron went onstage. It's hardly possible to make jokes these days unless you don't hurt anyone's feelings. This has a consequence of making most jokes boring as hell. Films like *The Naked Gun: From the Files of Police Squad!* (1988), *There's Something About Mary* (1998), or even my own film *Postal* could never be made again, which is a catastrophe. While horror is booming, there are no good comedies left.

Shortly before returning to the hotel, I went to a fast-food pizza store with Michael Roesch. As we stood at the counter, 6 black girls between the ages of 12 and 15 came out of nowhere and started beating each other up. The pizza maker ran into the middle and tried to separate the girls. He took one into the washroom and the others ran away. He came back, gave us our pizza, and said that this happened all the time. He was afraid that at some point one of them would come with a gun before too long.

I flew home and felt exhausted like I was in the wrong movie. I had to slow myself down and shake this challenging month off. Hopefully, what remains in *First Shift* is a good film, because the location, actors and camera were great. Ethan Maniquis (*From Dusk Till Dawn*, *Sin City*, *Machete*) edited the film and loved the material. The film was sold to Quiver for North America and released in June 2024. In Germany the film, the film came out around the same time.

While I was in NY, I got further rejections for projects from Netflix, ZDF, ARD, Apple, Amazon and Paramount+. Everything was going on as usual.

But the shoot was still fun, because, as with *BloodRayne* and other productions, bad luck and mishaps are, of course, the best and funniest parts when looking back on it. The many dinners I had with Gino, Kristen and Michael Roesch, and the actual creation of the scenes with the actors were great. The talent pool in NY is very large. I learned in conversations with Gary, Daniel, James, Willie, Kristen and Gino that they are all very unhappy with the quality of the productions that end up at their table. The TV productions that pay their rent are boring and full of clichés. They all had fun on *First Shift*.

A crew member said that no other director would have completed this film under these conditions, and I replied that I was the "worst director of all time" and therefore had no problem with such shooting conditions. I also had between 20,000 and 30,000 steps every night on my fitness iPhone app, so I saw filming as a free workout. It's a win-win situation.

BANDIDOS

During the Covid pandemic in 2020, I met with my friend Ralf Seeger, the German boss of the motorcycle club Bandidos for lunch.
Hells Angels and Bandidos are the biggest and worldwide known
outlaw motorcycle clubs in the world. Founded during the times
of the Vietnam War in the South, they are now present in over 50
countries with almost 8,000 members each. A lot of the violence
from these clubs involves fights against each other over control of
who has which territory. These clubs run casinos, brothels, swinger
clubs, hookah bars, security services and some real illegal dealings
with drugs, arms, and women. 90% of the members have normal
jobs, regular families, and have never been charged with a crime.

Documentaries have been made by ex-members giving interviews, but there has never been one involving acting members and
heads of the organization. I convinced Peter Maczollek, the founder
of the Bandidos in Germany, to let me film various meetings and
parties of the Bandidos and the World Run, which features over
4,000 Bandidos in Barcelona. We came closer to a deal, so I had
contact and talks with various members. Nobody was allowed to sit
down with me for longer interviews.

The head of the European branch of Bandidos was not so happy
about the idea of a documentary. Peter and his buddy Les didn't
want to give me an interview because in 2021 Les got into jail, and
they all got charged with ordering hits on people, building a criminal empire, and selling illegal weapons. The government seized
140 Harley Davidsons from them and 6 buildings, shut down half
of the chapters in Germany, and prohibited the Bandidos and Hells
Angels from wearing their jackets with their symbols and patches
in public. They had a hard time and weren't interested in my documentary.

I was able to film their trial. After a year, the judgement was that Peter got two years prison for illegal weapon ownership and Les for illegal weapon sales. Another guy got seven years for shooting thru a window at some Hells Angels. Evidence that they were running a criminal empire was non-existent or close to it.

In 2023, finally all of them agreed to do interviews with me. Now having loads of footage, we had our work cut out for us. The editing of the film took a long time, and I was the only financer. Netflix and other streamers were really excited about the documentary, but nobody offered any money for it. They were all scared and had fake ideas about what the Bandidos were.

They wanted me to make something like *Sons of Anarchy*, but I told them that I'm not dealing with actors. I had the real Bandidos filming with me. This was the first time they'd ever done something like this. I noticed that the big documentaries on the streamers only air after the trial has ended or the murder has been solved. They know where to put their cliffhangers at the end of each episode and how it all will end. After two years, I wrote an application to my hometown's film subsidies. To my surprise, out of the blue they gave me 30,000 euros. That motivated me along with 5.9 Filmproducktion who joined forces with me again after *Hanau* and *First Shift*. In January 2024, we finally sold the German speaking rights for Bandidos and delivered the completed 2-hour film.

RUN

My next film, *Run (2025)*, starts shooting in April 2024. It will be an action film about the migration crisis in Europe where every year over a million people come in by boat from Africa and the Middle East over to Europe. The boats almost always land in Italy, Spain, or Greece. From there, the migrants try to get into Germany, Austria, France, or the UK. My film takes place over the course of one day where a refugee boat arrives on the beach in a small tourist town. One of the refugees goes on a massacre which causes the whole city to take revenge on them.

There are too many migrants who cannot get integrated. A lot of them from Islamic countries don't want to integrate, but instead want to just get the social welfare money, free housing, and live in a parallel reality to where they came from. After Syria's civil war in Syria in 2015, migration has surged in Europe as has the crime. Germany takes in more asylum seekers than any other country in Europe. All of this is leading to more right-wing government members being elected because people are getting more and more fed up with the migrant situation. I was able to get Amanda Plummer (*Pulp Fiction* (1994)), James Russo (*Django Unchained* (2012)), Barhard Abdi (*Captain Phillips* (2013)), Sammy Sheik, Michel Qissi, Kristen Renton, Daniel Sauli, Costas Mandylor (*Saw IV* (2007)) Ulrich Thomsen, and Marcus Henderson (*Get Out* (2017)) for the lead parts.

AN OPEN WORD ABOUT THE INDUSTRY AND THE FUTURE

The entire film and TV industry is corrupt. Nobody in Germany gets funding or TV contracts unless they already have friendly contacts with the big decision makers. In other words, without the right contacts, you will never get a dime even if you are a good filmmaker and have great ideas. European subsidized films will always survive because they are completely paid for by taxpayers through TV fees and film funding agencies. Nobody wants to see these films, but that's how the cookie crumbles. Government budgets are planned and spent so that the jobs at TV and subsidy stations can be retained.

That's a big tragedy, but it's the truth. Many talents don't ever get a chance. Many idiots remain talent-free in the industry and shoot film after film. The subsidy-funded films are then shown at the film festivals. The independently produced films don't play at the festivals because the festivals are also getting subsidies to play subsidy films. One hand washes the other.

People like Dieter Kosslick, the ex-boss of Germany's biggest subsidy organization and the Berlin Film Festival, is a prime example of a highly acclaimed freeloader who lived all his life off government money. Many people live their entire lives at the state's expenses and never accomplish anything except throwing tax money out of the window for their lavish parties.

In European film, the real revenues from theatrical box office, DVD, or streaming Sales mean almost nothing because the typical producer will get millions from subsidies and free-TV sales before he starts filming. Producers pocket hundreds of thousands of euros off of each budget. They know the revenues later will be almost always nothing because home video and streaming revenues will be pennies on the dollar.

Less films are making money in the movie theaters than ever before. Most films with budgets between $1 and $40 million totally bomb. When *House of the Dead* made $11 million in US box office and *Alone In The Dark* made $6 million., everyone trashed them for making so little money. Now, more than 80% of all theatrical releases earn under $3 million in the US box office. The mid-budget film distributors are going under, and only the big studios and streamers will survive. Companies like Kinowelt, Senator, Wild Bunch, Splendid Films, and Open Road Films are only artificially kept alive by investors, but they are not really making any money. If these companies can no longer get loans or investments from billionaires, they would all be bankrupt tomorrow.

In the film business, ego plays an incredibly important role, even though no one wants to admit it. Most decisions in business and politics are not made by common sense but instead are made by ego with greed and sex as the driving forces, which are then presented to the public with made-up reasons and bullshit excuses. Unfortunately, that's also the reason why people and not countries start wars and revolutions. Ego supports politics by using up all the resources to ruin the environment so that no one can live on earth 80 years from now. Any reasonable person would say, "They are all going crazy? How can we allow all this shit?" Many people have these thoughts, but they have no real power to really change anything. It is like the old phrase, "It is the end – the question is only when!"

For a time, I didn't see my future in films anymore but in political activities. I dove into politics not only in my YouTube videos and my podcast Uwe Boll Raw but also even going so far as attaching myself to political parties. I gave up trying to be a political leader because all the parties follow only their agendas and are all corrupt.

Now, I focus more on animal welfare. I just sent a donation to PETA and sued chicken-laying batteries that still simply shred chicken. When it comes to animal protection, you could still cry all day long: seals are still being mauled in Canada, monkeys and dogs are still being killed in tests by the cosmetics and pharmaceutical industries, dolphins and whales are being harpooned by the Japanese, and so on! In Germany, factory farming has hardly changed. I gave a good friend of mine some money to drive into Ukraine during the war to rescue animals from there.

We live in a world whose pollution/CO2 emissions are too high, and we know it. All scientists warn us about the consequences of consumption. We see more and more tornadoes, rising sea levels, and the simultaneous drying out of entire states like California. The mentality has spread that we can no longer reverse the process. All the poles, Antarctica, and Greenland will melt completely, and the sea level will rise by 10 meters within in the next 80 years. That would be the end for almost all cities that are at sea level, but also for countries like Holland, Bangladesh, and many others. Billions of people must relocate or die. This will lead to chaos and tragedy.

At the same time, humanity is developing backwards and seeking refuge in idiotic religions. More wars and conflicts are breaking out, mostly due to religious fanaticism mixed with a very uneven distribution of wealth. Islamist fighters spread fear and terror with terrorist attacks. Politicians try to keep their positions, but do not really try to improve or change the situation. No politician wants to tell the people how bad things really are, and their half-baked solutions in no way delay the downfall. It's like on the Titanic where the band continued to play until the ship was already half underwater.

I'm 58 years old now, and, as you can see, time flies quickly. If I can give you, dear readers and especially young filmmakers, some advice, consider the following:

Never spend all of your money on a film or go into debt for it. Instead, work with a positive cash flow. Never count money that might come as your income.

Always try to use a limited liability company (LLC) and never hold liability yourself because films pose a great risk of unforeseen lawsuits.

Look into the film market, and don't make a movie that's outside of it because film is an expensive hobby (and that's exactly why it's not a hobby).

No viewer is interested in any topic if it is not presented in an entertaining and believable way. You can make films about any topic, but, above all, make it entertaining.

Go your way, and make sure that you can always look in the mirror and be at peace with yourself.

Your future is not easy at all, but it is worth fighting for.

A LOOK BACK

In Germany, representatives of the New German Cinema such as Rainer Werner Fassbinder, Peter Schamoni and Volker Schlöndorff initiated film funding 40 years ago by calling for new and different films. "Grandpa's cinema is dead," they said. That was the end of the commercial driven German Cinema with great films of all genres, the films that everyone still watched and that my generation grew up with. At that time, film funding institutions emerged on every corner in every German federal state, which to this day primarily serve to create jobs for those working there at state expense. It now has an annual spend of 3 billion euros in state funding every year. Most of that money goes to only 100 people or companies who then fill their pockets without any real control of success.

In Germany, you, must submit applications and get approvals before filming. That doesn't exist in Canada. In Canada, you will receive around 30% of the labor costs back, no matter what film you make. If I spend $100 on a gaffer in the province of British Columbia, I get around $30 back. This is the Labor Tax Rebate. This applies to every film no matter how big or small the budget. I can shoot whatever I want, and I get that portion of the money back if I spend the money on film work.

The heads of German film funding are not interested in such a model because then all the staff positions would disappear. If the Canadian model were implemented, administrative costs would fall to around 20 million euros per year (far less than the hundreds of millions they spend now), and significantly more money would be available for the films. The way funding works in Germany can be equated with nepotism in socialist systems. By the way, cultural censorship is also practiced because everything that is controversial, hard, dark, realistic, or cruel is prevented by the broadcasters and funding.

The result is that, with very few exceptions, German films are not sold in foreign territories and are only shown in Germany. Less than 5% of the films supported annually make their money back through theatrical and foreign sales, and over 50% of the films do not generate any theatrical or sales revenue at all.

My old production partner Frank Lustig wrote his master's thesis about the plight of film funding in 1994, and nothing has changed since then. Of the 90 German films funded in 1992, 43 films sold no tickets and another 20 films sold less than 10,000 tickets.

Between 1991 and 1993, the Filmstiftung NRW under Dieter Kosslick supported 90 cinema projects with 75 million DM. Only 16 of them were even released in cinemas. Such a disastrous track record should have led to the film foundation being abolished! Instead, the funding continued to increase over the years with Kosslick being appointed head of the Berlinale Film Festival.

Two decades later in 2015, there was an evaluation of film funding within the framework of the Film Funding Act (FFG) by Prof. Dr. Dieter Wiedemann. It was carried out on behalf of the Association of German Cable Network Operators, the Bitkom Federal Association for Information Technology, Telecommunications and New Media. Prof. Wiedemann's evaluation found the same results as Frank's thesis. Even 20 years later, hundreds of millions are sunk into films without reaching an audience. In addition, Frank Lustig found that of 194 screenplays funded between 2009 and 2013, only 44 were actually filmed. The market share of German films was always only between 16.8 and 27.4%, although there were only around five successful German films per year (almost always comedies) which basically accounted for 80% of sales. A whopping 95% of the films flopped or didn't even make it to the cinemas.

Because of the millions in funding, there are too many films overall that neither the market nor the TV stations need. The number of moviegoers has fallen almost every year for the past decade. From 1960 to today, the number of moviegoers has fallen by over

65%. Wiedemann is calling, among other things, for a reallocation of funding so that 80% of the money is only distributed as reference funds. In essence, this means that 80% would be distributed to those who have produced successful films. The idea is not bad, but of course it keeps all newcomers away from funding. To make a successful film in the first place, one needs to get funding to begin with!

In my opinion, funding and TV have to be looked at together and need reform. Otherwise, nothing will change in terms of nepotism and corruption. The Canadian model based on the motto "I spend $100 and automatically get $30 back" would mean that all funding agencies could be dismissed, and all producers would have planning security and the same playing field. This would save Germany over 300 million euros per year. Yes, you would still have to raise money to make a film, but the corruption would end, and the competitive advantages of the established companies would be gone.

The real analysis that Wiedemann or the Federal Audit Office, the Office for Large Business Audits and a public prosecutor should provide would have to be based on the following questions:

Which companies have received money for what projects from funding and TV stations over the last 30 years?

How much money did companies receive from funding and TV stations?

How often was additional money paid for consultations, project developments, extras, and overruns?

Were there any donations from producers to TV editors or film funding employees in the form of gifts, money, work lunches, art, wine, or? All receipts, cash withdrawals, checks, and credit card statements should all be audited!

The funding usually takes the form of a conditionally repayable loan. How much money did the producers have to pay back? Have proceeds been properly accounted for?

Disclosing this information would be fatal to many careers. While pensioners in Germany have to recycle bottles to earn money to survive, the subsidy support staff fly business class to film premieres and festivals. Directors and producers drive around in Jaguars when, based on their work results, they should be traveling by bus. Germany will hardly be able to secure pensions in the future. What we have here is a savings opportunity to invest tax money more sensibly than before in areas that really need it like funding to help children and elders out of poverty.

In the film funding scene, public prosecutors and politicians should have been investigating this for a long time by now. In the style of a landowner, money is given out by loons who prove with their daily productions that they don't have any idea of what quality really is. Just so that you, dear readers, can see what I'm talking about here, here are a few concrete examples from thousands of cases:

Luigi Falorni (a director you don't have to remember) received 1,043,000 Euros in funding for his film *Feuerherz* (2008). It sold 2,732 tickets; eight times less than what we sold with our 30,000 euro film *German Fried Movie*. This means that each ticket was subsidized by the tune of 523 euros per ticket sold. After it was a total cinema flop, the DVD launch was also supported with more taxpayer money. I'm guessing that Luigi still has thousands of DVDs in his basement, and all his friends get this masterpiece every year for birthday and Christmas presents.

Mike Eschmann's *Morgen, ihr Luschen! Der Ausbilder-Schmidt-Film* (2008) received an incredible 1,444,000 million euros in funding with an additional 89,000 euros on top of that for distribution. In the end, only 5,263 tickets were sold at the box office. These are subsidies not unlike those given to the opera, coming out to 291 euros per ticket.

We must also not forget the nonsense *Everyone Has A Plan* (2012) by the Argentinian Director Ana Piterbarg, which was funded with 720,000 euros and selling a mere 3,167 tickets, proving that she really had no plan at all! I wonder whether Wim Wenders has even paid for a flight to a festival or an overnight stay in a hotel himself in the last 20 years.

There is funding tourism, and the darlings of funding are hyped everywhere. At the Cannes Film Festival, they show their own series of German films financed entirely by taxpayers' money. No one wants to see them in Cannes except the Germans who fly there at taxpayer expense. When I was in Cannes in the past, I saw them all sitting on the terrace of expensive hotels. Hans Wolfgang Jurgan, the Degeto managing director at the time, was later fired because of questionable business practices with all the other film promoters. They would throw lavish dinners with wine and lobster. Because they didn't have to earn the money themselves, they happily threw it out the window without any inhibitions.

Because it's so beautiful, another prime example… Fred Breinersdorfer is still proud of his 49 viewers for the ten-time Oscar winner (just kidding!) *Zwischen heute und morgen* (2009). The subsidy per viewer on this one comes out to 5,061 euros.

The selection of the Hessian funding 2020 is also sensational where you no longer have a chance at all with normal stories. For example, *Lesbian City Ideas* by Jules Bieber and Lena Mittelbach was supported as it was politically correct. The same goes for the films of Joanna Bielinski for having "strong and controversial female characters, feminist themes".

First, they make films that no one wants to see. The film funding agency ensures that this shit is shown worldwide by the Goethe Institutes and placed at film festivals as part of a special series, all of which are completely paid for by the German taxpayer. My film *Hanau* was rejected by all nine sections of the Berlinale because they thought it is more important to show films about Chilean beekeepers and fly the filmmakers in than showing an unfunded German film that deals with the largest racist massacre in the history of Germany.

My films *House of the Dead* and *Alone in the Dark* have grossed more money on DVD and in cinemas than 80% of the German films funded in the last 40 years combined (this comes out to around 35,000 films)... And yet, I get they give me no funding for my films.

According to Section 2, the FFA's tasks, paragraph (1) 4, the FFA (Film Promotion Agency) states:

"The FFA has the task of establishing the international orientation of German filmmaking and the basis for the distribution and market-oriented exploitation of German film domestically and its economic and cultural aspects to improve broadcasting abroad."

Didn't I do that more than any other German director?

I have made 36 films with a volume of over 400 million euros, almost all of which were sold in over 100 countries and were exploited in all media in these countries. I am one of the very few German directors who is known worldwide.

In Germany, there is no competition for success, there is only competition for funding and TV funding. The production companies which receive the most money from the funding are often economically linked to the public broadcasters through investments and maintain other subsidiaries with different names.

Based on my own experiences plus the research results, it is completely clear to me that the German funding system and public television have mafia-like structures. Because of the concrete daily actions of editorial teams and committees, public funds are misused and embezzled. Bribery, abuse of office and expenses, corruption and incompetence are part of that system, encouraged by the arrogance, ignorance and completely wrong self-assessment of the editorial snots working for the public TV and subsidy stations.

In 2022, thanks to journalistic investigations, scandals in the BR (500 million euros in retirement savings gone), NDR (political influence on the editors) and RBB (director Schlesinger lived like a god in France with private chefs, massage chairs in the company car and having an expensively renovated office, etc.) were disclosed to the public. The ARD broadcasters spend around 160 million euros a year on their directors, including offices, employees, broadcasting councilors and expenses, while ZDF spends almost 50 million euros.

Since a lot of money and possible crimes are involved here, I hereby call on the public prosecutor's offices to investigate and house searches all broadcasting stations and at the heads of funding and juries, TV directors, editorial and department heads at home. Only then can the full extent of the matter be known of possible embezzlement as well as possible cases of bribery, abuse of office, taking advantage of office, fraud, tax evasion, and theft come to light. My motto for this is as follows: Don't just turn over the basements of entrepreneurs and threaten them with pre-trial detention, but also hold officials and institutions financed by the state or taxpayers accountable.

In addition to the above-mentioned possible crimes, it is also about distortion of competition and market manipulation. Anyone who is not accepted by around 100 editors and funding juries has no chance in Germany. Those who are accepted become richer and richer, even without actual economic success, because everything including script writing, production preparation, production, post-production, distribution, festival participation, and receiving the German film awards is paid for by the taxpayers and the state. This makes any real assessment or self-criticism unnecessary. As long as the jury or editorial team gives the movie or TV series a thumbs up, like Nero in the gladiator fights of old, you can live in the lap of luxury. The damage caused by funding and public broadcasters over the last 40 years is over 40 billion euros. This makes other spending scandals look like pittance!

I am the only German film director who has had an international career in spite of the will of the government subsidies and TV stations in Germany and has survived financially without them.

When I came back to Germany in 2020, I gave it another shot and submitted around 20 projects in different genres for both myself and other directors. One script was written by Peter Jamin, a best-selling author who has worked for WDR for years, and Günter Adnan Köse, an experienced director who has received critical acclaim for other projects. Even this project was denied! Of my 20 projects, at least 5 would have been funded if they had been submitted by one of the companies who regularly get funding.

It's important to note that I don't want to condemn the production companies here, because they do what they must to get money. They develop projects and try to finance them any way they can. It's quite logical that they want to gain a competitive advantage by getting on good terms with TV editors and funding juries. It is these editors and juries who allow themselves to be lulled and corrupted, thereby betraying their actual task and committing numerous crimes. It is their job to remain neutral, to give all producers the same opportunities and care and to finance or co-finance the best, most promising productions.

The record of German film clearly shows that this system does not work. Due to this structure, German film is economically and artistically below average internationally. It has been a feel-good and self-enrichment store for around 100 editors, producers, and jury members for more than 40 years now. The fact that the state (including the federal states) is willing to continue to hand over more than 3 billion euros a year to this limited circle of people in times of over-indebtedness, inflation and recession is no longer acceptable.

In North America, more and more states try to make it more attractive to shoot films. Michigan, Georgia, California, New York and others compete with their own subsidies. Some production companies have already abused these systems with inflating production costs.

The reason why entertainment companies are reporting losses is based on the failed idea that streaming will be a cash cow for all of them. Instead, streaming has destroyed the home video and theatrical business. They cannot compensate for these losses with subscriber revenues alone.

10 years ago, the audience knew that if they didn't watch a film first in the theater or bought or rented a DVD or watch it on pay-per-view, then they would have to wait over 6 months to watch it on premium channels like HBO and SHOWTIME.

My $7 million dollar film *House of the Dead* made $11 million in box office but also $28 million in home video revenues. To make a DVD, it costs $1 per disc, but they are sold for $14.99 apiece in stores. The profit margin on DVDs was very high. The revenue from the home video market saved a lot of films and kept the business going. The key to making films work for decades was having a traditional theatrical window. Now this is all over! The only winner for now is Netflix who gathered enough subscribers around the globe to make money. Only 10 movies a year released in theaters make substantial profits, and most of the other films don't even recoup the release costs. Hundreds of films get on the silver screen only to qualify for an Oscar run or to get some traction to earn more money for the streaming rights.

At the same time, production costs are getting higher and higher. Movie stars are getting paid absurd amounts for TV series or direct to streaming movies. Since films no longer go through all the distribution windows anymore, they vanish after three weeks completely from the New Release section into the abyss of their gargantuan back catalog.

Years ago, I wrote an article with the headline "There Is No Money in Movies". It started with a press release about 4Kids Entertainment and Legendary Pictures. Let's look at it as an example:

4Kids Revenue Plunges

NEW YORK: 4Kids Entertainment has reported fourth-quarter revenues of $4.8 million, down from $16.2 million in the year-ago period, with a net loss that was reduced from $21.3 million to

$7.4 million. For the entire year, revenues fell from $34.2 million to $14.5 million, while net loss was reduced from $42.1 million to $27.2 million. 4Kids says it will "take all actions it deems necessary to preserve its business and assets, including the potential filing of a petition under Chapter 11 of the United States Bankruptcy Code.

Legendary Pictures announced they need another $900 million line of credit.

What I want to say is film companies operate with money that was made in the REAL world, meaning in other industries. Rich people invest in banks, hedge funds, and film companies. Years later, after they learned that there's no money in movies, they write them off. It is amazing to see that the stream of movies is not stopping. Likewise, the stream of loans and hedge funds money into film production companies is still not ending. This just shows that some people make so much money in their real business (computers, oil, pharma, real estate, etc.) that they still can afford to piss money in the wind in making movies.

In the end, film companies that file for bankruptcy DO NOT PAY ANYBODY THEIR MONEY BACK. Of course, the management still gets great salaries years after years. Then, the same managers flanked by great PR open new companies and again ply the money market and with enough drugs, parties, prostitutes (meaning young actresses) and bullshit business plans to make another credit facility give them cash flows again.

Theaters are a lot of time filthy, unclean, and loud. Cellphones are ringing and people are crunching their popcorn loudly during the whole movie. The theaters do NOTHING to help independent films grow. They play only the trailers of the huge event tentpole movies that have big banners and standees outside the movie. The in-theatre advertising is the most important, but the movies that need it the most don't get it. Theaters must show also more trailers for smaller movies. The theaters did not help any distributors to save some money in advertising, and they don't support small movies. They kick out almost all the movies after two or three weeks, so it's very hard to get word of mouth that will allow a smaller film to grow into a hit.

The fact is that for under $40 million in P&A for a big domestic release on around 3,000 screens, you cannot reach public awareness to make an opening weekend of $30 million or more. Over 80% of the movies with only $20 million or below in P&A will not make even $15 million in total box office. This means you will have net only $7.5 million theatrical revenues after spending $20 million on a theatrical release.

Based on these disastrous theatrical revenues, the studios and anybody else are forced to try to shorten the windows and get money out of every outlet at almost the same time.

Let's look at some more facts:

In 1990, you could make a big movie for $10 million and release it big for only $5 million in P&A. Nowadays, a medium budget movie costs $75 million and the US release would require $40 million in P&A. How can you release a medium budget movie if nearly every week you are competing against a $200 million movie spending $100 million P&A on 6,000 screens?

In the old days, you had 5 to 10 big budget event movies per year. Now, including the animated movies which cost over $100 million apiece, you have 45 event movies. This model has destroyed the medium budget movies. This isn't because big budget films are any good! Instead, it's because they are so expensive and need to spend so much money in P&A to win their weekends and market share.

Even if the major film studios are now omitting their medium-budget product and go only for event movies, they are still losing money. If they spend $150 million on making a big movie and spend $70 million in P&A for USA/Canada only, they would need to earn $440 million box office in USA/Canada alone to recoup this movie. Only 10 to 15 films per year ever pull that off.

The so called "word of mouth" movies are major setups like *Borat* (2006), *Black Swan* (2010), *The King's Speech* (2010), *The Fighter* (2010), and horror films from Blumhouse spend a minimum of $30 million in P&A per movie. The Oscar-nominated films also have major P&A spends; for example, *There Will Be Blood* was over $42 million.

If a major company makes a profit in their film unit, it is due to booking costs in other departments (TV rights, direct to streaming, etc.) so that their profitable TV stations make less profits. In paying $50 million for the US TV rights for a movie, you help the film, but damage the balance sheet of the TV Channel.

The audience clearly goes only to movies with the biggest advertising campaigns. This is why all the independent distributors cannot be successful: they have smaller movies, less P&A, less press, and no support from the exhibitors.

It's proven that actors are totally overpaid. Some big action stars get hyped up for saying only five lines of dialogue a day while they let the stunt guys do the hard work. If the studios would overall not pay more than $3 million at most per big star in a movie, the stars would work for that price if nobody else would ever offer any more than that. It's also absurd to pay medium star names more than $250,000 per film. Since the streaming wars have started, medium names are getting $500,00 or more per episode.

Film unions are not helpful in a market where everything is in the toilet. I am not talking about TV here, but just the independent film market. Why can't a waiter in LA. work as extra or actor for $50 a day on a major movie or sell his script for $5,000? It's better to get less money when you start working in the business you want to work in because you already have a day job. Why should producers pay 5% to SAG and WGA from their box office gross if their movies are only making half of their money back. Actors and writers are getting paid upfront, so why are they also getting gross points? Who thinks about the investors?

Why are streamers paying $20,000 for independent movies but spending between $50 to $200 million per film or TV series for their own in-house productions?

The majors must agree to reduce the P&A because it makes their movies unprofitable. If nobody spends more than $20 million for P&A, then the box office for everything will be on a level playing field because people will want to see all these movies.

The press, TV, and radio must report more on small films, otherwise the public will never know they exist.

What is with all the totally arrogant and overpaid agents, managers, agents and studio executives in L.A. living in hot-air balloons? If I ran a studio, I would do the same movies for half of the production costs by throwing the cokeheads out and cutting the bullshit breakfast, lunch and dinner meetings with idiots who have never made a movie in their life. I can shoot a movie like *The Fantastic Four: Rise of the Silver Surfer* (2007) in half of the time for half of the money with each shot being exactly the same.

2023 WGA & SAG-AFTRA Strikes

In 2023, the WGA followed by SAG-AFTRA went on strike. It was the largest strike the film industry has seen in 40 years! As you might guess, I have some thoughts on the topic.

What is really wrong, unfair, and absurd in the film industry in the first place? While the strikes went on, the film, TV, and streaming industry in North America was basically at a standstill. Active productions dropped more than 80% as soon the writers went on strike. They were later joined by the actors. The attempt of the studios/streamers to scan actors digitally and use them as they like in future productions is a real threat to the actors' survival. This is especially true when you think about this in tandem with the refusal of the streamers to pay real royalties/residuals to the actors in the first place.

However, I also feel that all parties included are missing and overlooking some important facts. They all have not really been willing to see what the real situation in our industry is. Time to list some facts up front to open up a wider discussion and ask for more honesty from both sides.

Right up front, way more people merely think they are in the film industry. Out of the 160,000 SAG members and 11,500 WGA members, only about 20% of them are making enough money from the film industry to support themselves full-time. The other 80% have to work other jobs or are supported by their parents. This is not counting the at least 100,000 actors and 50,000 writers who are not part of SAG-AFTRA or the WGA. In LA, every dentist thinks he is a screenwriter, and every Uber driver and waiter thinks they are an actor. As far as crew members (IATSE), it's different because an AC or grip are 99% of the time making a living from their jobs and not delusional like most of the actors and writers are.

The majority of studios and streamers are actually not making money… In fact, they are losing money and believe that having a better market share will solve their problem, but it won't. If producers could get perfect scripts written by AI and have absolutely 100% real looking digital avatars playing parts instead of real live actors, it is of course very compelling to do productions this way if it gets cheaper to make things on computers. If you don't need actors or writers, you also don't need crew, equipment and location rental, catering, honey-wagons, airplane tickets, studios, props, hotels and per diems because there will no shooting films on real sets with real actors anymore. Everything can be done with just a producer, director, and a staff of CGI technicians. In big studio films like *The Avengers* (2012), *Transformers: Rise of the Beasts* (2023), *Indiana Jones and the Kingdom of the Crystal Skull* (2008), the real-life actors only show up for the dialogue scenes. In all the action scenes, they just put their faces digitally on the stuntpeople or their CGI clones. So, if you could tell Chris Hemsworth for *Thor 5* that you don't need him in-person at all for the next film, but you still wire him $10 million instead of the $30 million if he would shoot the film himself, then it's a WIN WIN for the actor AND the studio. But, if you tell the extras that they will be paid $580 for one time to play an actor and going forward their digital likeness can be used in every Marvel movie going forward without any extra pay, then it's only a WIN for the studio. All of this is scary for everyone who works in the film industry because it could be the end of their income and of film production as we know it!

Now comes the hard part of my open letter. This is why my career and life went totally different to any other filmmaker or producer. If you go ask around in Hollywood about me, then you will get mixed answers. A lot of people will say that I got bad reviews, made bad films, and fought my critics in a boxing ring for real. These are all people who have only seen 3 or 4 of my films (*Alone in the Dark, House of the Dead, In the Name of the King: A Dun-*

geon Siege Tale, BloodRayne, Far Cry) of my 36 films, googled me, and regurgitate what other geeks wrote. You also find some people who know and love my films not based on the video games, but the political, and, by the way, dead on, films like *Rampage, Assault on Wall Street, Stoic, Postal* or *Darfur*.

What is more important for me is something else entirely. I owe nothing to nobody, and I own all my films. Neither my company nor myself ever went bankrupt. My company also has been debt free for 33 years. A lot of famous people I hired in the beginning of their careers: Elisabeth Moss (*The Invisible Man* (2020)), Julian Clarke (the editor of *Deadpool*), Nate Parker, Sam Levinson, and many more. All the people I worked with from PAs to Jason Statham got paid on time and know how fast and professional I ran my shoots. I never went over budget with a film. Everybody who worked on an Uwe Boll film loved it because in over 1,000 shooting days for all my films combined, I had only 10 days with overtime. I could have stopped working 10 years ago, traveled the world, and called it day, but I love making movies. I care not for Bentleys and other bullshit the rich and famous spending their money on, so I will keep on making films.

A lot of Hollywood producers and distributors are just in it for the money and defrauding filmmakers and investors. CEOs take bonus money out of the pot, not out of profits. Companies who are almost bankrupt still pay high amounts of money out to management.

When video rentals tanked and Blockbuster went out of business, Netflix came and saved the industry. All creatives always go where the jobs and money are. All of the directors, producers, actors, and crew jumped happily into business with Netflix and all the other streamers. They loved it because they got 100% financing including decent producer's fees. If you produce something independent, only 1 out 10 productions break even. All producers know that, so they compete like crazy to get orders from streamers. Netflix gets at least 5,000 scripts per year to pick from. If nobody wants them, scripts are overall mostly worthless.

The streamers overpay some celebrities (Obama, Prince Harry) and mega-producers like Shonda Rhymes, the Russo Brothers, Ryan Murphy who are only mega-producers because they get so much money. Really, they had maybe one or two hits and then got flooded with money. As soon they have those deals with the streamers, they get huge offices, hire all kinds of people, get Lakers season tickets, and fly on their private jets to Save the World conferences or Beyoncé concerts.

Netflix and the other streamers underpay for productions they acquire in markets like AFM. It's totally unfair to producers and filmmakers who work for a year, make a good film, and then get 100K as a license fee from a streamer who gives other producers $10 million to make an original movie that is not necessarily better than the acquired film. If the streamers would pay more for licensed films, they would save the independent film world.

Streamers tend to promote their expensive originals like crazy, so everybody clicks them on and a few weeks later they claim, "Hey, *Citadel* is a big success!". But is it really? A mediocre CGI-driven $280 million trainwreck? Would anybody pay money to see something like this in a movie theatre? Wasn't *Beef* or *Athena* ten times better than *Citadel* or the other ten $200 million budget direct-to-streaming disasters like Sense8?

The A+ actors are totally overpaid, and they know it. They are lucky to be in franchises, and the studios are so stupid to think that the actors have real value. The agents for these actors make sure that all non-franchise films they do still have budgets over $100 million so that they can get a $20 million salary for their clients. They also know the studios will promote the shit out of those films. They think for whatever reason that their stupid productions like *The Avengers* or *Indiana Jones and the Dial of Destiny* (2022) are better if they are at least three hours long. These monster productions are slowly but steadily losing fans and box office. To release *Barbie* (2023) alongside *Oppenheimer* (2023) only one week after *Mission: Impossible - Dead Reckoning* (2023) came out cost the latter up to $300 million in worldwide box office. When I was young, we just had three or four of these big films coming out per year (E.T. the Extra-Terrestrial (1982), *Star Wars: Episode IV – A New Hope* (1977)), but now every week brings one mega film after the other. Nobody wants *The Flash* (2023), *Ant-Man and the Wasp: Quantumania* (2023), or *Venom: Let There Be Carnage* (2021). They all still make good box office but only because nothing else gets proper advertising money behind it. Only the big films getting all the in-theater advertising (trailers, talk show promotions, tv spots), so the audience goes for the popcorn films like lemmings and forgets what a good film really is.

This scenario is the death of good films. The films my generation grew up with *Taxi Driver*, *The Godfather*, *Apocalypse Now*, *The French Connection* (1971), *Rocky*, and *Dances with Wolves*. The films that have won Oscars in the last 10 years like *Moonlight* (2016), *Birdman* (2014), *La La Land* (2016), *Everything Everywhere All at Once* (2022) are jokes in comparison to films like *Goodfellas*, *The Deer Hunter* (1978), *Born on the Fourth of July* (1989), *Platoon*, *Reds* (1981), *A Clockwork Orange* (1971) or *One Flew Over the Cuckoo's Nest* (1975).

The studios mostly believe only in comic book and other franchise CGI-driven films. They aren't spending big money on anything else. Smaller but better films written for adults are mostly now only on streamers where they disappear after one week. Back in the day, films in video stores were on the shelf for three to six months and gained traction over time. Later, they would get more viewers when they aired on cable and other TV outlets.

Big name actors are getting the wrong advice. The only independent films they do is with their buddies. All film festivals only invite films with the big-name actors in, even if the films are totally shit. The last 10 Terrence Malick films all had big names. These actors didn't even get it that staring at the stars, waves or cornfields does not make a good film. They are too stupid to see that a lot of hyped-up filmmakers have nothing to say.

If my film *Attack on Darfur* had an A-list star in it, it would get nominated for various Oscars. Watch it for free at this streaming link and see if I'm right:

https://vimeo.com/253469446

Password: Dafuer

At the end of the strike, it looked like the studios and streamers had lost and the WGA and SAG had won. Actors and writers are now getting AI protection and 20 to 40% more money. Just a few months later, we saw a drop in productions of around 30%, which was clearly going to happen. The already strong-booked people making more from the other 90% who barely got booked are now losing 30% of their shooting day and income and can be finally Uber drivers or waiters again.

The A-list actors need to bleed and cut their absurd salaries by half to free up money for others who really need it. Hey, Di Caprio, you remember *What's Eating Gilbert Grape* (1993)? That was the last time you didn't phone it in! That was before your super yacht was more important than your craft. Robert Downey Jr., you remember *Natural Born Killers* (1994)? You all can save the film industry by acting in gritty, edgy, realistic, political films because then these other productions will get funded and promoted, and the audience will learn how to appreciate real films again. Right now, if you replace real actors with their digital avatars, you are not damaging the film industry any more than the industry has already damaged good films.

Best Regards,
Dr. Uwe Boll
Bolu Filmproduktions- und Verleih GmbH
March 30, 2024